Developing Reading
Comprehension

THE UNIVERSITY OF
WINCHESTER

Developing Reading Comprehension

Paula J. Clarke, Emma Truelove, Charles Hulme
and Margaret J. Snowling

Illustrations by Dean Chesher

WILEY Blackwell

This edition first published 2014
© 2014 John Wiley & Sons, Ltd

Registered Office
John Wiley & Sons, Ltd, The Atrium, Southern Gate, Chichester, West Sussex,
PO19 8SQ, UK

Editorial Offices
350 Main Street, Malden, MA 02148-5020, USA
9600 Garsington Road, Oxford, OX4 2DQ, UK
The Atrium, Southern Gate, Chichester, West Sussex, PO19 8SQ, UK

For details of our global editorial offices, for customer services, and for information
about how to apply for permission to reuse the copyright material in this book please
see our website at www.wiley.com/wiley-blackwell.

The right of Paula J. Clarke, Emma Truelove, Charles Hulme and Margaret J. Snowling
to be identified as the authors of this work has been asserted in accordance with the
UK Copyright, Designs and Patents Act 1988.

Library of Congress Cataloging-in-Publication Data
Developing reading comprehension / Paula J. Clarke [and three others] ; illustrations by
Dean Chesher — First edition.
    pages   cm
  Includes bibliographical references and index.
  ISBN 978-1-118-60676-6 (hardback) – ISBN 978-1-118-60675-9 (paper)
1. Reading comprehension.   2. Reading comprehension–Study and teaching
(Elementary)   I. Clarke, Paula J.
  LB1573.7.D46 2013
  372.47–dc23
                                                        2013029204
A catalogue record for this book is available from the British Library.

Cover image: Mary Ethel Hunter, Girl Reading, oil on wood. Leeds Museums and
Galleries / The Bridgeman Art Library
Cover design by Design Deluxe

Set in 11/13pt Arial by SPi Publisher Services, Pondicherry, India

1   2014

Contents

List of Figures

List of Boxes

Foreword by Jean Gross CBE

In my two years as government's Communication Champion for children I described the Reading for Meaning project and its findings everywhere I went, as an example of how working on children's oral language impacts on their achievement in reading. And every headteacher, literacy leader and SENCO immediately asked how they could find out more about an intervention that clearly meets a pressing need in schools – what to do about children who towards the end of primary school are not on track to meet the attainment levels required by the age of 11.

Schools and teachers know the central importance of reading comprehension for success in English. They also know how much it matters for grasping the meaning of word problems on maths papers, and for learning right across the curriculum. Yet there is a huge gap in our knowledge of what to do to enable children who are poor comprehenders to catch up with their peers.

This book helps to fill that gap. It will be of interest to every primary teacher and leader, providing, practical guidance on how to develop the components of comprehension. The book describes small group intervention programmes. The ideas – such as invaluable advice on how to develop children's spoken vocabulary – have however a much wider application and should be used in every primary classroom, every day.

Even more importantly, the ideas are based on sound evidence. As educators, we are getting better at using evidence from research. We are beginning to use the language of trials, control groups, statistical significance. This book will take us further on that journey. The teaching strategies it describes, such as distributed practice, scaffolding and co-operative learning, are firmly rooted in evidence. They form the design principles of the Reading for Meaning intervention programmes, which in turn were subjected to full Randomised Controlled Trials. The researchers followed up children's progress well beyond the end of the intervention period. They can demonstrate that the interventions worked, and that (particularly for the oral language intervention), the impact did not 'wash out' when the additional support ended.

Finally, the book makes a significant contribution to our understanding of the reading process. It provides further support for the 'Simple View of Reading' and reminds us of the importance of language comprehension as well as decoding skills. It is one of a long line of publications from a group of researchers who have made an outstanding and sustained contribution to our understanding of how children learn to read, and of what for me has always been of vital importance – how to help those who can't read well.

Jean Gross CBE, founder of the Every Child a Reader initiative and former government Communication Champion for children.

Acknowledgements

In preparing this book we are very grateful to Tanya Cowton and Fiona Richards for providing the teaching assistant commentary. We also wish to recognise the contribution of our illustrator Dean Chesher, who has created all of the figures, boxes and illustrations in the book, and Emily Reeves who compiled the index.

Many individuals have contributed to the success of the project and we would like to thank all children, parents, teaching assistants and schools for their co-operation, hard work and participation.

We are particularly grateful for the help of Elizabeth Fieldsend, who was key in supporting our teaching assistants, and Sarah Watson who made a significant contribution to the project in its final year through dissemination activities and data analysis. We would also like to give thanks to Angela Harrington who wrote some bespoke passages for the intervention programmes.

We would like to thank the research staff who helped us at different stages of the project including, Claudine Bowyer-Crane, Pamela Baylis, Kimberley Manderson, Silvana Mengoni, Dimitra Ioannou and Leesa Clarke. Furthermore we would like to recognise the contributions of support staff including Geraldine Collins and Simon Fletcher and the many students who helped with data collection and preparation of teaching materials.

Chapter 1

What is Reading Comprehension?

Language conveys meaning and allows the sharing of information, ideas and perspectives. When written messages are successfully understood, reading can be a wonderfully inspiring, enjoyable and transforming experience. Written language has the power to take the mind to different places, times and events; it can put us in the shoes of fascinating characters and hold our attention through gripping plots, suspense and intrigue. Texts can provide escapism and offer alternative perspectives on the world; what's more, they can 'kindle' our imaginations to create rich mental images that may stay with us forever. Texts can inform and develop knowledge, provide us with new vocabulary and provoke new ways of thinking.

For many children, however, the messages conveyed through written text are not well understood; this has potentially far-reaching consequences for their learning, development and well-being. This chapter outlines the richness of written language and the complexities of the processes involved in reading for meaning. This serves to highlight the many ways in which children's ability to understand text can break down, and will provide points to consider when teaching and developing interventions to improve reading comprehension. Chapter 2 considers in more detail the difficulties that cause some children to have specific difficulties in understanding what they read.

To consider the richness of written language, let us consider the following short passage as an example:

Developing Reading Comprehension, First Edition. Paula J. Clarke, Emma Truelove,
Charles Hulme and Margaret J. Snowling.
© 2014 John Wiley & Sons, Ltd. Published 2014 by John Wiley & Sons, Ltd.

Jennie sprang bolt upright. Moments of disorientation followed before she recognised the now faded floral wallpaper and tatty matching curtains. Framed family faces stared down from the bookshelf. 'Home for the holidays' she remembered. Blinking and yawning she stumbled around for her slippers and gown. The tinny voice from the bedside table was delivering the news and warning of harsh winds and icy roads. Jennie reached across and hit the button. 'Today is definitely a two sweater day,' Jennie thought as she rifled around in her suitcase for her favourite winter clothing.

Reflect for a moment on your understanding of the passage and think about the following questions:

Why did Jennie spring bolt upright? Where was Jennie? Why might she have felt disorientated? What are the framed family faces? Why did she stumble? Where was the tinny voice coming from? What was the button? What did Jennie mean by a 'two sweater day'? What was Jennie doing in her suitcase?

Returning to the passage, consider your experience of trying to decipher its meaning. In the annotated version in Figure 1.1 we have documented some of the initial reflections that you may have when you reread the passage.

The complexity of comprehension is highlighted in these annotations. Engaging in this type of conscious 'think-aloud' activity focuses attention on aspects of reading comprehension that might otherwise go unnoticed. In the example, you can see that our understanding of the text's message gradually builds up over the course of reading it. Initial predictions are confirmed by later information, potentially ambiguous vocabulary is resolved by the context and assumptions based on previous experience are tested. The annotations, however, only scratch the surface of the demands of the task. Making connections between parts of the passage in order to build up an interpretation requires recognition of the words, an ability to hold information in mind, an ability to scan backwards and forwards to relevant words and phrases, an understanding of cues from sentence structure and punctuation, an empathy with the character and many other skills and processes.

Only part of the task of reading comprehension is situated within the text itself; a developed understanding comes from the interaction between the text and the reader's response to it. The diverse perspectives that we bring to the task result in different interpretations of a text. When we watch films of books that we have read they rarely match up to our imagined versions. When we discuss reading material

Jennie sprang bolt upright.
- Maybe Jennie is surprised, in shock or has woken up suddenly? Something has caught Jennie's attention.

Moments of disorientation followed
- She may be feeling confused? She could be somewhere unfamiliar?

...before she recognised the now faded floral wallpaper and tatty matching curtains
- These were once in good condition, now they look worn and they may be less recognisable.

Framed family faces...
- The only faces that I can think of that are in frames are in photographs or paintings.
- These may be images of Jennie's family?

stared down from the bookshelf.
- Unlikely to be real faces in frames as it is not possible for people to fit on a bookshelf.

"Home...
- The use of this noun further suggests that the family faces are from her family.

...for the holidays" she remembered.
- The feeling of disorientation coupled with the thought that she is there for the holidays suggests that this is not her everyday home.
- I link this to my experience of spending time at my parent's home during the holidays.
- I consider that this may be the family home that Jennie grew up in.

Blinking and yawning...
- This suggests that she has just woken up.

...she stumbled around
- She may still be feeling disorientated or still slightly sleepy which may cause her to be less co-ordinated when trying to find these items.

...for her slippers and gown
- Presumably a dressing gown rather than a ball gown or graduation gown?

The tinny voice from the bedside table...
- Tables are inanimate, and do not have mechanisms for conveying sounds so the voice is not actually from the table.
- Rather it must be from something on the table.

...delivering the news and warning of harsh winds and icy roads.
- 'Tinny' makes it sound like it is being transmitted rather than a real voice. News can be transmitted by the radio or television or telephone.
- Radios are often part of alarm clocks and are used to wake people up.

Jennie reached across and hit the button.
- Buttons you hit are usually on machines rather than clothing. These can be used to turn things on or off.
- The button could be on an alarm clock.

"Today is definitely a two sweater day"
- Sweaters are an item of clothing; two of these would be warmer than one.
- This suggests that she is going to wear two to keep warm because of the cold weather mentioned in the news report.

Jennie thought as she rifled...
- 'Rifle' when used as a verb means to search. This is a more likely interpretation than the noun 'rifle' which is a gun.

...around in her suitcase for her favourite winter clothing.
- As it is cold and she is looking for winter clothes it suggests that the holidays that she is home for are in the winter, so may be Christmas or New Year.

Figure 1.1 An annotated version of the sample passage demonstrating the results of a think-aloud activity

with others, we may find that we have interpreted the same sentence in very different ways. We may also find that our interpretations are inconsistent with the message that was intended by the author. Such differences in imagination and personal response, whilst complex and difficult to capture, are at the heart of the reading comprehension experience.

MODELS OF READING COMPREHENSION

Models of reading comprehension can help us to understand the different skills and processes involved in interpreting text. The simple view of reading (Gough and Tunmer, 1986) offers a useful model for characterising successful reading. As shown in Figure 1.2, Gough and Tunmer (1986) propose that two skills are needed in order to read for meaning: the ability to recognise or pronounce the words (decoding) and the ability to understand spoken language (listening comprehension).

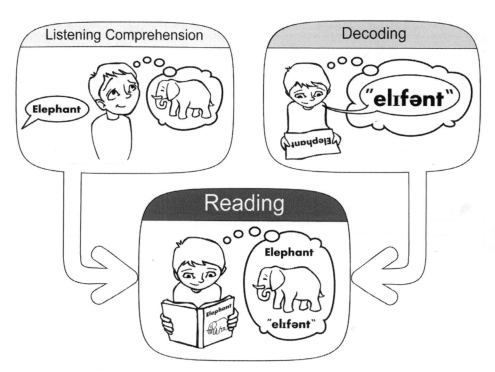

Figure 1.2 The simple view of reading (Gough and Tunmer, 1986)

As well as helping us to understand reading success, this model can help to describe the different ways in which reading can break down and inform early identification and intervention for children at risk of reading difficulties. According to the simple model, a child may show a generally poor reading profile and experience difficulties in developing both decoding and listening comprehension. Alternatively, a child may have difficulties in the area of decoding but show intact or even superior listening comprehension skills. The opposite pattern to this, termed 'the poor comprehender profile', is also possible and will be the focus of the next chapter. This profile is characterised by intact or superior decoding skills coupled with weak listening comprehension. As a result, children with a poor comprehender reading profile will read aloud well but have difficulty understanding what they read. Children who experience difficulties with decoding, listening comprehension or both skills will experience difficulties in understanding text.

Another model that can be used to capture the skills and processes involved in successful reading is the Construction–Integration Model of Kintsch and Rawson (2005). This model, presented in Figure 1.3, provides a more detailed overview of the processes involved in reading comprehension. The model proposes that when we read text we create a personal representation of its meaning; this representation (or mental model) is made up of the information from the text itself alongside our general knowledge of the words and the topic.

The processes involved in deciphering the text are described in terms of three levels. The first is the 'linguistic' level in which the reader recognises and processes individual words and their meanings. The second is the 'microstructure' in which the reader goes beyond words in isolation to recognise and process the meaning of larger chunks of text. The third is the 'macrostructure' in which the reader recognises and processes themes, topics and genre information about the text. These three levels form what is called a 'textbase'. The textbase combines with the reader's existing general knowledge to form an individual's representation of the meaning of the text. This interpretation is called the 'situation model' and, in forming it, the reader uses many different types of knowledge. For example, the reader may need to use theory of mind skills to understand the author's or character's intentions, beliefs, desires and feelings. To have a 'theory of mind' requires an awareness of your own mind, recognition that other people have minds and an understanding that another's mind is independent of your own. This understanding provides the foundation for perspective taking and the realisation that others have ideas and emotions which may be similar to or different from your own.

1. Linguistic

The reader recognises and processes individual words and their meanings.

For example:
'Disorientation'

Baffled, Bewildered, Puzzled, Confused, Unsure...

2. Microstructure

Work at the sentence or phrase level in which the reader goes beyond words in isolation to recognise and process the meaning of larger chunks of text.

For example:
Moments of disorientation followed before she recognised the now faded floral wallpaper and tatty matching curtains.

The reader understands that the character temporarily feels confused as objects around her are initially unfamiliar. The wallpaper and curtains do not look as they once did so the reader understands the character has seen these objects before.

3. Macrostructure

The reader recognises and processes themes, topics and genre information about the text.

For example:
Jennie sprang bolt upright. Moments of disorientation followed before she recognised the now faded floral wallpaper and tatty matching curtains. Framed family faces stared down from the bookshelf. "Home for the holidays" she remembered.

The reader connects their understandings at the microstructure level to infer that the story is based around themes of home, holidays and family. The reader identifies the genre as likely to be fiction based in real-life.

Figure 1.3   The Construction–Integration Model (Kintsch and Rawson, 2005)

Textbase

This represents the meaning of the text derived only from information expressed by the text.

General Knowledge

The reader draws on their own general knowledge about holidays in the past involving the home and family members.

This general knowledge may be drawn from a variety of experiences including those personally encountered, those read about, those seen on television and so on.

Situation Model

For a deep understanding of the text, the reader goes beyond the textbase to incorporate general knowledge and thereby reach a personal and emotional representation of what has been read.

This draws on their 'theory of mind' skills. In our example, the reader may think about they feel when visiting family. They may also consider what preparations they make at holiday times and consequently what the character might be thinking about or planning whilst on their visit. The reader may think about a time when they felt disorientated and remember how that felt.

Figure 1.3 (*continued*)

To illustrate the application of this model, we can link its features to the processes involved in understanding the passage introduced at the beginning of this chapter. Let's remind ourselves of the passage:

Jennie sprang bolt upright. Moments of disorientation followed before she recognised the now faded floral wallpaper and tatty matching curtains. Framed family faces stared down from the bookshelf. 'Home for the holidays' she remembered. Blinking and yaw[ning] she stumbled around for her slippers and gown. The tinny voice from the bedside table was delivering the news and warning of harsh winds and icy roads. Jennie reached across and hit the button. 'Today is definitely a two sweater day,' Jennie thought as she rifled around in her suitcase for her favourite winter clothing.

By following this example through, you can see how an apparently simple passage can be understood at several different levels, all of which contribute to the formation of a rich situation model.

Taken together, these models describe many of the skills and processes involved in reading comprehension. However, it is important to remember that models are not 'real' – they are theories that may be incomplete or incorrect in a variety of ways. Such models can be tested and refined in research into how people read. Consideration should also be paid to other aspects of reading not specified in these models, for example the relationship between understanding text and motivation. When we read something that we understand and can immerse ourselves in, we are motivated to read more. Enjoyment of text promotes engagement and sustained interest and attention. If comprehension breaks down reading will be less pleasurable, which may lead to less time spent reading, which in turn will weaken reading skills further.

It is also necessary to recognise the metacognitive skills that underlie reading for meaning. Metacognition refers to what we know about our own knowledge and includes the ability to reflect on our understanding of text as it unfolds. As we saw in the 'think-aloud' activity at the beginning of this chapter, there are many aspects of reading comprehension that can be dissected and reflected upon. As individuals, we vary in our ability to keep track of what and how much we understand. Some people may think frequently about their interpretation of a text both during and after reading, whilst others may monitor less and may continue to read on, long after they have lost the thread of the story or passage. The extent to which an individual monitors their own understanding may also vary according to the reason why they are reading. For example, if you have been asked to prepare for an exam, you may read more intently and with more emphasis on understanding than if you are flicking through a magazine in the dentist's waiting room. This aspect of reading for meaning is often referred to by the term 'standard of coherence'; that is the degree to which an individual is concerned with whether text makes sense.

Perfetti, Landi and Oakhill (2005) argue that for reading comprehension to develop, a high standard of coherence is necessary. To give an example, Sophia and George are two children with different standards of coherence. When reading a story, they may extract the same level of meaning but while Sophia classes this as unclear, George considers it is satisfactory and therefore does not seek further clarification. Sophia is likely to be better able to develop good comprehension because she deploys a number of strategies to gain further information that will enable her to overcome the feeling of not fully understanding; these may include asking an adult or a peer a follow-up question or thinking back to a similar personal experience and bringing her previous knowledge to bear. George, on the other hand, may read on without the sense that he has not fully extracted the meaning from the passage.

THE IMPORTANCE OF READING COMPREHENSION

At this point, it is necessary to return to the importance of reading for meaning. Much of the commentary surrounding theoretical models of reading comprehension has focused on the knowledge that the reader brings to the process of understanding. However, it is important to recognise that reading can be a transformative experience influencing the thinking and learning of the reader. New words, concepts and perspectives can be encountered that challenge and enhance existing knowledge. Consequently, reading is central to teaching and learning and it is vital to consider the circumstances in which the developing child is required to extract and apply meaning derived from text.

Reading comprehension skills become more important as children progress through the educational system. Teachers frequently expect children and young people to research topics from books or from the internet in the Sciences as well as the Arts and Humanities. Indeed, in all areas of the curriculum children need to be able to locate relevant information, to filter out the information that is less pertinent to the current topic and to select the appropriate information to focus upon. For example, maths comprehension exercises draw upon reading comprehension skills to support the development of numeracy skills. Consider the following:

> *The local primary school was having a cake sale to raise money for charity. John baked two dozen buns. Anita made ten brownies but two were too burned to be sold. Before the sale, John dropped half a dozen buns on the floor which his dog promptly ate. In total, how many baked goods did John and Anita bring to the cake sale?*
>
> Answer: 26

Having read this chapter, you will no doubt recognise the number of comprehension processes and skills involved in completing this calculation. For example, a number of vocabulary items are crucial to understanding the question including 'dozen', 'brownie', 'baked goods'. Furthermore, the child must understand the preposition 'before' in order to correctly sequence the events in the question. Thinking back to the Construction–Integration Model, the child is likely to be assisted by accessing general knowledge and previous experience of baking and attending cake sales. A child's success in understanding the question at the levels of words, sentences and overall gist will impact on the cognitive resources available and capacity to attend to the key mathematical calculations required. This is just one example of how reading comprehension skills support and influence learning in areas that are not generally associated with literacy.

Box 1.1   TA commentary

Maths is definitely an area where I have worked with children who are unable to decode the question, and therefore are unable to provide an answer until the question is either read out to them or rephrased in a manner that they can understand. The simple act of reading a SAT's paper question to them may be all that is needed to enable them to concentrate on the maths and not the reading.

SUMMARY

When we read we seldom pay attention to the complex processes that contribute to our ability to understand text. In this chapter we have considered the inherent complexity of reading for meaning. In doing so, we have made reference to key theoretical models and component skills and processes. In this book we will consider the skills that are involved in learning to read with understanding, how and why reading comprehension may break down and what characterizes a 'poor comprehender'. Against this backdrop, we describe in detail a project that we undertook to develop and evaluate a set of interventions to develop reading comprehension in children in the middle school years. We will present findings that demonstrate the efficacy of these interventions and elaborate their content for practitioners who wish to use them. We will argue that such interventions should be part of the 'toolkit' of teachers, teaching assistants, special needs advisors and speech and language therapists who are concerned with individual differences in children's literacy.

Chapter 2

The Poor Comprehender Profile

Reading is a highly complex process and therefore it may not be surprising that some children struggle to become proficient readers. As outlined in Chapter 1, children with the poor comprehender profile demonstrate weaknesses in understanding what they read despite being able to read aloud accurately and fluently. Poor comprehenders' strengths in decoding often mask their difficulties in comprehension and, as a result, such children are likely to go unnoticed in the classroom. This may be especially true during the early years of schooling when emphasis is placed on learning to decode. As the teaching emphasis shifts from 'learning to read' to 'reading to learn', children who struggle with aspects of understanding what they read become increasingly disadvantaged. The ability to access text is crucial for supporting learning across the curriculum and communication through writing increases with age; thus, reading comprehension difficulties are a considerable obstacle to educational attainment.

The long-term implications of weak comprehension make it important to raise awareness of the poor comprehender profile among parents, teachers and educational professionals, and to ensure that children who are affected receive support as early as possible. Our understanding of the poor comprehender profile has increased markedly in recent years. In practice, the criteria used to define the poor comprehender profile are not fully agreed and the cut-off used to define an impairment is to some degree arbitrary. Furthermore, the assessments used to measure

Developing Reading Comprehension, First Edition. Paula J. Clarke, Emma Truelove, Charles Hulme and Margaret J. Snowling.
© 2014 John Wiley & Sons, Ltd. Published 2014 by John Wiley & Sons, Ltd.

comprehension vary considerably. As a consequence incidence rates have been reported to range from 3 to 10% of primary school aged children.

The difficulties experienced by poor comprehenders become apparent from around 8 years of age when the mechanics of reading are secure. Although comprehension weaknesses at this age may be relatively mild in comparison to those experienced by peers with special educational needs, there is evidence to suggest that poor comprehenders are unlikely to catch up and will continue to have difficulties. Indeed, there is a concern that as children transfer to secondary education the emphasis placed on 'reading to learn' across subject areas may lead to widespread difficulties for poor comprehenders across the curriculum. For these reasons we believe that poor comprehenders are deserving of extra support during primary school to prevent a spiral of negative outcomes over time.

Box 2.1   TA commentary

Comprehension is such a vital skill that it leaves children at a disadvantage in all subject areas. Poor comprehenders are less able to use information that is provided in lessons to help with class work or struggle to understand the instructions that are given to them, either printed or given verbally. Teachers frequently expect children to research topics from books and the internet. Some children are unable to filter the relevant information and are therefore unable to select appropriate information to use.

Figure 2.1 illustrates the poor comprehender profile, which is characterised by the discrepancy between the ability to read words aloud accurately (a skill which is usually within the average range) and the ability to answer questions which tap understanding of what has been read (a skill which is usually below average).

It is important to note that, although the Simple View of Reading promotes the idea of separating the ability to decode and the ability to comprehend, in reality it is not possible to fully disentangle the two skills. Reading comprehension assessments typically allow the examiner to assist the child with difficult words during the assessment (and thereby support the child's decoding) in an attempt to gain a purer measure of the child's understanding of the passage. This procedural aspect of the tests is helpful; however, the two skills remain highly interrelated.

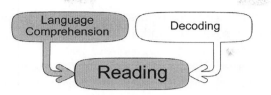

Figure 2.1   The 'poor comprehender profile'

FACTORS THAT CONTRIBUTE TO POOR READING COMPREHENSION

As discussed in Chapter 1, there are a multitude of processes involved in reading for meaning (e.g. it is necessary to remember and manipulate information, to know what individual words mean and to be motivated to understand). Not all of the processes involved can be easily measured by a comprehension test. Consequently, the factors influencing a child's score on a reading comprehension measure (on a given day) may be different to the factors influencing another child's score, even though they both may be classed as 'poor comprehenders'. For example, Sabrina has difficulty connecting ideas in text and doesn't enjoy reading, whereas Adam loves to read but struggles to remember story events and often doesn't realise when his understanding is breaking down. This is one of the reasons why the poor comprehender profile should not be considered a diagnostic category; rather, it is a behavioural profile that may reflect a range of different underlying problems that compromise the ability to develop adequate reading comprehension skills.

There is much evidence to suggest that children with a poor comprehender profile also demonstrate difficulties across a number of other areas of learning. The research indicates that possible areas of difficulty include language skills, working memory and text-level processes (such as inferencing and comprehension monitoring). However, it is unlikely that a given child will show weaknesses in all of these areas. In short, there are likely to be multiple factors influencing the poor comprehender profile and it may be the influence of several factors that leads to weak reading comprehension skills in any individual.

Language Skills

Spoken language provides the foundation for reading and so it is essential to consider the relationship between reading and language skills in order to understand why children show the poor comprehender profile. Language skills can be divided into four areas: phonology (the sounds of the words), semantics (the meaning of the words), grammar (the structure of words and sentences) and pragmatics (the social use of language). By definition, poor comprehenders show strengths in the development of phonological skills as demonstrated by age-appropriate reading accuracy and fluent reading aloud. However, other aspects of language are closely linked with comprehension and a number of studies suggest that the wider language skills of poor comprehenders are impaired. We will focus on what is known about the poor comprehenders' language profile in relation to the meaning of words and the structure of words and sentences since, at the time of writing, studies that have considered the role of pragmatics in the poor comprehender profile are rare.

Understanding the Meaning of Words

Perhaps unsurprisingly a child's understanding of individual word meanings is closely related to their ability to understand connected text. Understanding word meanings is often measured by a child's ability to define vocabulary items. For example, we could ask a child 'What is a shoe?' and get a sense of the richness and quality of the child's under-standing of the word by scoring the spoken definition they provide. Text comprehension relies on being able to access word meanings efficiently and integrate them into the context of the passage.

Nation and Snowling (1998a) found that poor comprehenders were much slower and less accurate than peers in judging whether two words shared similar meanings (e.g. CRY–SOB) but they were equally accurate and only very slightly slower at deciding whether two words rhymed (e.g. ROPE–HOPE). This finding led them to suggest that a general problem with word meanings is one underlying difficulty for children with the poor comprehender profile. Following on from this, Nation, Snowling and Clarke (2007) investigated the idea that poor comprehenders have particular difficulties learning new words. They taught poor comprehenders and normal readers of the same age the names of artificial objects (e.g. 'a corbealyon is a small, hairy, angry bird') and then tested their understanding of the words by asking chil-dren to recall the definition of the word and produce the name of the object when given the definition.

The following day children were asked to remember the words and then match them to the correct pictures. Poor comprehenders learned the new items as quickly as typical readers but found it much more difficult to provide definitions for the new items. Furthermore, a day later they found it harder to recall the meaningful parts of the objects. These findings were confirmed by Ricketts and colleagues (2008), who provided evidence to suggest that poor comprehenders can make links between new words and their meanings, but the stored word meanings are not as deep and robust as those of their peers. The reasons for this are unknown, but children who know fewer words may also find it harder to learn new ones because they cannot make as many links with existing word meanings; this means that children's difficulties with word meanings can be compounded over time.

When reading connected text, knowledge of word meanings is only helpful when it is successfully integrated into a representation of the meaning of the passage being read. Nation and Snowling (1998b) assessed how well poor comprehenders could use context to support their understanding of sentences. To investigate this, they compared poor comprehenders with children with dyslexia and typical readers of the same age. They found that all three groups were supported by context but the effect for children with the poor comprehender profile was reduced. In a later study, Nation, Marshall and Altmann (2003) tracked the eye movements of poor comprehenders whilst they were reading to test the idea that these children were less sensitive to the context of sentences. They found that poor comprehenders were just as skilled at making eye movements to the important contextual parts of the sentence as their peers. However, the patterns of eye movements were different; poor comprehenders tended to make many short glances at the target objects whereas typical readers made fewer and longer looks at the important contextual information. This pattern suggests that poor comprehenders are equally sensitive to context but have difficulty in remembering or attending to important information. In line with this interpretation, we explore the influence of working memory later in this chapter.

The majority of research conducted in this area has primarily involved children who have English as their first language. However, in practice many children communicate using multiple languages and there is a need to understand the reading comprehension skills of these learners. A study by Burgoyne and colleagues (2009) investigated the reading comprehension, listening comprehension and vocabulary skills of 46 children with English as an additional language (EAL) alongside 46 monolingual peers. After accounting for differences in reading accuracy, they found that monolingual children had higher levels of text comprehension than children with EAL. In addition, the vocabulary skills of children with EAL were significantly lower and this was found to be a significant predictor of reading and listening comprehension. The findings of this study highlight the importance of vocabulary and have implications for meeting the needs of these learners; children with EAL may benefit from interventions to support comprehension, such as those considered in this book, but further research is needed to confirm this.

Understanding the Structure and Organisation of Words,
Sentences and Connected Text

The meaning of a sentence, and even the individual words within it, are often affected by the order of the words. For example, in the following statement who was bitten and who was chased?

The cow that bit the dog was chased by the zebra.

A secure understanding of the grammatical properties of sentences supports children in understanding what they read. Additionally, children's understanding of structure and organisation can help them to detect errors in their reading and monitor their ongoing understanding more carefully. The relationship between grammatical understanding and reading comprehension has received less attention from researchers who are interested in the language profile of poor comprehenders; however, there is some evidence to suggest children with a poor comprehender profile struggle with the grammatical structure of language.

Nation, Clarke, Marshall and Durand (2004) looked at the oral language skills of 25 poor comprehenders aged seven to nine years and compared them with peers matched for age and decoding skill with comprehension in the average range. Children's grammatical understanding was assessed by asking them to recall complex sentences, to change verbs into the past tense and to select the correct picture to match a spoken sentence. In addition, children's semantic skills were assessed using two tests that involved asking children to define words and to explain why words go together. The results showed that the language skills of children in the poor comprehender group were weaker than children in the control group in every area except those involving phonological aspects of language (the sounds of words). Furthermore, eight children in the poor comprehender group (but no children in the control group) met the criteria for specific language impairment, indicating that some poor comprehenders experience severe language difficulties. The authors concluded that weaknesses in broader (non-phonological) aspects of language place a constraint on the development of reading comprehension skills.

In line with this, and pulling together all the evidence, we suggest that poor comprehenders could also be classed as poor *language* comprehenders. Several studies highlight difficulties in both the semantic and grammatical areas of children's language development. However, what is unclear from the studies discussed so far is whether weak language skills precede poor reading comprehension or result from lower quality and possibly less frequent reading experiences.

Early Indicators

As reading comprehension difficulties tend to emerge around eight years of age, it is hard to disentangle the relationships between reading and language because by this point oral language and reading skills have been developing together and affecting each other for some time. An important longitudinal study by Nation, Cocksey, Taylor and Bishop (2010) addressed this issue by examining the early language and reading profiles of poor comprehenders. They carried out assessments of reading and language with 242 children aged five and assessed their progress at four further time points during the next four years. When children reached eight years of age, 15 of the original group were classified as poor comprehenders. By comparing these children with 15 skilled comprehenders of the same age, they were able to look at the pattern of strengths and weaknesses in the poor comprehender group over time. They found that children displayed the characteristic poor comprehender profile of reading skills from age six when they began to read passages. Decoding and phonological skills developed appropriately; however, the raw scores obtained by poor comprehenders in reading comprehension showed remarkably little change between the ages of six and eight. When Nation and colleagues examined the early language profiles of these children, they found that non-phonological oral language difficulties were present at age five before the development of reading skills. Poor comprehenders displayed persistent mild-to-moderate weaknesses in understanding spoken language, providing word definitions, recalling sentences and in the grammatical understanding of sentences at all ages. This study provides evidence to suggest that the oral language weaknesses of poor comprehenders are present before reading skills develop and are not a consequence of problems with reading comprehension.

Thus, early oral language difficulties may place children at risk of future weaknesses in reading comprehension. These findings are consistent with others that show that early oral language skills are good predictors of later reading comprehension skills. This conclusion is of educational significance as it opens up possibilities for the implementation of early intervention strategies that emphasise preventative rather than remedial support for children with weaknesses in understanding what they read. To date the interventions developed to support poor comprehenders have targeted children in mid-childhood after they have been identified as having weaknesses in comprehension. Indeed, this is true of our own intervention study, which is the focus of this book. Nevertheless, the importance of developing early language intervention is underscored and our group has recently shown that early oral language intervention can improve the development of reading comprehension skills in the early years (Fricke *et al.*, 2013). The first book in this series, *Developing Language and Literacy*, provides more information about early language intervention.

Working Memory

The term 'working memory' refers to the ability to hold information in mind while simultaneously performing other attentionally demanding activities. Working memory processes may be important for text comprehension, because reading involves holding information in mind about what has just been read while continuing to decode upcoming words and to integrate this new information with what has gone before. It follows that a possible cause of reading comprehension difficulty is a working memory problem.

A variety of tasks have been used to investigate the working memory skills of poor comprehenders. In one classic working memory task (listening span) a child hears a series of short sentences and is asked to decide if each one is true or false. At the same time, the child is required to remember the final word from each sentence and, after a sequence of sentences have been presented, to recall these final words in order. Poor comprehenders find this task tricky. The task shares many similarities with real life language comprehension in which language must be held in mind, manipulated and acted upon. For example, in the classroom, poor comprehenders are likely to struggle with multistep instructions or lose the thread of a story they are narrating.

Working with Text

Let us move on to consider two high-level skills that are related to working directly with text: inferencing and comprehension monitoring.

Making Inferences

The ability to draw an inference and thereby link pieces of information together in a text is critical to successful reading comprehension (see Chapter 1). Children must not only integrate information in a piece of text but they must also use their knowledge of the world to support understanding.

Cain and Oakhill have carried out a body of research that shows that poor comprehenders have difficulties in making links between information in text. In one study (Cain and Oakhill, 1999), they examined the relationship between young children's reading comprehension and their ability to make inferences. The researchers compared poor comprehenders with skilled comprehenders (of the same age and with matched reading accuracy) and younger children who have the same reading comprehension levels as the poor comprehenders (comprehension age-matched group). This younger group was included to test the direction of the relationship between inferencing and reading comprehension – the recurring question of which one leads to the other? Children were asked to read four stories and afterwards answer questions that tapped two kinds of inference: inferences that link pieces of information within the text (text-connecting inferences) and inferences that use general knowledge to support understanding (gap-filling inferences). The ability to make these inferences was compared with the ability to answer questions about literal information that was clearly stated in the text, thereby requiring no inference.

Cain and Oakhill found that poor comprehenders struggled to make both types of inference when compared to the other groups; however, they were equally good at answering questions about literal information. Younger children with the same level of reading comprehension ability were better at making text-connecting inferences than the poor comprehenders. This led the authors to suggest that poor reading comprehension does not lead to poor inference making (because otherwise both groups would have had the same inference-making skills); rather, they believe that difficulties in making inferences, at least partly, contribute to the difficulties poor comprehenders have in understanding what they read. Cain and Oakhill (1999) also wanted to find out whether poor memory could explain the difficulties poor comprehenders experienced with inference making. They concluded that poor memory could not wholly explain difficulties in inferencing. They offered another explanation. They found that when prompted to make inferences, poor comprehenders were able to do so and therefore they suggest that poor comprehenders might be focusing more on word reading than on monitoring their comprehension of the text. In this way, skilled comprehenders might have a different reading strategy to poor comprehenders; they may be aiming to gather a complete and coherent picture of text as they read whereas poor comprehenders may aim to decode the text accurately and not know when to bring their general knowledge to the text.

Monitoring Understanding

When reading, our thought processes continuously monitor our understanding and feed this information back into the reading process. This high-level process is known as 'comprehension monitoring' and there is some evidence that poor comprehenders are less successful at engaging in these checking processes during reading.

Oakhill and colleagues have investigated the comprehension monitoring ability of poor comprehenders. Oakhill, Hartt and Samols (2005) asked nine to ten year old poor comprehenders and a matched group of good comprehenders to detect errors in stories. Errors were either word-level errors or sentence-level errors. For example, a word-level error was presented in the sentence 'a bitterly cold wind' by replacing the adjective 'bitterly' with the made-up word 'ferly' and children were asked to find the incorrect word in a sentence. Alternatively, a sentence-level error would involve reordering words in the sentence 'all Joe had to do was sit there' to the incomprehensible 'all was there sit had to do Joe'. Skilled comprehenders were better at resolving sentence-level errors than poor comprehenders but the two groups performed similarly on word-level errors. A follow-up study examined the influence of working memory by comparing performance on a working memory task with another error detection task. This time the two groups were asked to detect two sentences in the story that had contradictory meanings. For example:

Moles cannot see very well, but their hearing and sense of smell are good.

Moles are easily able to find food for their young because their eyesight is so good.

Again, the poor comprehender group performed less well at detecting these contradictory sentences than the good comprehenders. What is more, the further apart the sentences were in the text, the greater the difference in performance between the two groups. This provides more evidence to suggest that poor comprehenders struggle to monitor their understanding of text. The poor comprehenders also performed more poorly on a working memory task; however, despite working memory being linked to comprehension monitoring, it could not fully explain the results of the error detection task. Together these findings suggest that comprehension monitoring contributes to reading comprehension ability in its own right (not just because it involves working memory). Oakhill and colleagues suggest that poor comprehenders are unable to build rich mental models of the text they are reading and this in turn affects their ability to monitor comprehension. The more complete and integrated the overall mental model of the text, the more likely a child is to detect errors and this may account for some difficulties shown by poor comprehenders when working with text.

In Chapter 1, we introduced the term 'standards of coherence' to express the idea that children have different standards for determining whether something has been understood. According to Perfetti and colleagues (2005), a high standard of coherence is necessary for the development of good reading comprehension skills. What is more, the standard of coherence held by each child is shown by how much he or she reads with the aim of understanding, makes inferences and actively engages in comprehension monitoring. We know that poor comprehenders have difficulty in inferencing and monitoring their understanding; however, more research is needed to understand the standards of coherence held by poor comprehenders. It is likely that children with reading comprehension weaknesses have lower thresholds for deciding what makes sense. Whether standards of coherence come before or after difficulties with reading comprehension is an important question to answer; however, it is likely that over time the two will exert negative effects on each other.

ENVIRONMENTAL INFLUENCES

Children who are less able to understand what they read are more likely to disengage from reading. The enjoyment children derive from books is pivotal in their motivation to read and thereby practise their developing skills. As outlined in Chapter 1, motivation and enjoyment are key influences on the development of reading comprehension skills. Motivation to read can be linked to a number of environmental influences including teaching methods, reading at home and exposure to a range of books. Sénéchal (2006) conducted an interesting study that considered the role of reading experience in the home. She found that children whose parents focused on letters, sounds and learning to identify printed words tended to develop decoding skills more quickly than children whose parents emphasised interaction around language during reading; however, the second group of children tended to have enhanced reading comprehension skills.

Given that comprehension is the goal of reading we feel that it should be given equal attention to decoding when children are learning to read and particularly as children begin reading to learn. There are a number of reasons for highlighting the importance of comprehension; perhaps the most significant is that engagement with meaning is more likely to sustain motivation and thereby increase the time children spend reading. This is sometimes referred to as the 'Matthew Effect' (Stanovich, 1986). The 'Matthew Effect' refers to how there can be a spiral of positive outcomes for children who enjoy reading and then choose to read more both in school and at home. For poor comprehenders, we need to do all we can to develop and sustain their enjoyment of reading and so counter the potential spiral of negative educational outcomes that were discussed at the beginning of the chapter.

The importance of environmental factors sets the scene for the rest of this book, which outlines teaching approaches for supporting reading comprehension. The evidence for these teaching programmes is highlighted through an overview of our large-scale research project in Chapter 3. Details of the teaching principles that underlie the approaches can be found in Chapter 4 and details of the intervention materials in Chapters 5, 6 and 7. These chapters pull together what is known about effective methods of teaching children about reading for meaning through stimulating packages of intervention. Although these packages of intervention were implemented in school, we see no reason why the principles for teaching and some activities could not be transferred to instruction at home. If we consider the importance of environmental factors in the home (as demonstrated by Sénéchal, 2006) it is likely that using consistent teaching methods at home and school will support children to an even greater extent.

SUMMARY

In this chapter we have offered an overview of the research around a group of children who have a reading profile known as the 'poor comprehender' profile. Based on the simple view of reading (Gough and Tunmer, 1986), this profile highlights the needs of children who have good skills in decoding words and sentences (so can read aloud at an age-appropriate level) but struggle to understand what they read (so have weak comprehension skills). We have considered the importance of meeting the needs of this group of children to avoid the potentially widespread adverse effects of poor reading comprehension on learning and motivation throughout these children's school lives. In relation to this, we have highlighted the important role of environmental influences including motivation, instruction and exposure to reading material. In addition, we have considered in some depth the processes that may underlie the poor comprehender profile, including language skills, working memory, inferencing and comprehension monitoring. We believe the evidence shows a very close link between children's language comprehension skills and their ability to understand what they read. Links between language and reading comprehension have strong implications for early intervention in which a preventative rather than remedial approach is advised. The first book in this series outlined a similar intervention project for young children entering school and provides information and resources regarding early language intervention, which you may find useful. Figure 2.2 outlines the possible areas of difficulty

Possible area of difficulty	Possible presentation in the classroom or at home
Vocabulary	• May use limited or repetitive vocabulary in speech and written work. • May use words incorrectly indicating a lack of deep understanding of word meaning.
Oral Expression	• May struggle to organise and express thoughts and ideas clearly. • May reduce participation in class-based activities such as question and answer sessions.
Figurative Language	• May take language at face value and attribute only a literal meaning. • May find jokes and word play confusing.
Narrative Skills	• May struggle to tell others about experiences outside of school in a way which makes sense to those listening. • May find it difficult to sequence a story effectively and establish a coherent plot.
Grammatical Development	• May struggle to understand complex sentences and work out who did what to whom. • May experience difficulties with structuring sentences.
Verbal Reasoning	• May find it challenging apply reasoning skills to language. For example, may find it difficult to think about words which have similar or opposite meanings.
Inferecing	• May fail to link two ideas together if the link is not explicitly stated. • May predominantly accept literal meanings. • May not refer to relevant background knowledge when encountering new concepts.
Comprehension Monitoring	• May continue with activities without an awareness of not having understood important pieces of information.
Verbal Working Memory	• May find it difficult to follow multi-step instructions in class. • May complete the first instruction in a list and then struggle to know what comes next. • May need constant reminders.
Motivation to Read	• May dislike or avoid reading. • May choose to read a narrow range of books.

Figure 2.2 Possible presentations of the poor comprehender at home and in school

for children with a poor comprehender profile and how they may be recognised in the classroom or at home.

This list is neither exhaustive nor prescriptive; we do not claim that all these difficulties will be seen in children with the poor comprehender profile and nor do we suggest that only children with the poor comprehender profile will display such difficulties. The table is intended to provide a useful guide for highlighting areas of learning that may contribute to difficulties in reading comprehension. Perhaps when reading this chapter you have had a child or group of children in mind. If so, you may find the table useful as a means of indicating whether or not the children would benefit from the teaching programmes that are at the heart of this book.

Chapter 3

The York Reading for Meaning Project: An Overview

Over the last decade, our understanding of the nature of the difficulties experienced by children with the poor comprehender profile has increased greatly. However, we still know relatively little about how to prevent the development of these problems or how best to help older children overcome such problems. Most intervention studies have evaluated single strategy interventions. Recognising that reading comprehension can break down for a variety of reasons we believed that a package comprising teaching activities targeting multiple components of reading comprehension should be developed and evaluated. Furthermore, whereas most previous studies have employed research staff to implement interventions, we wanted to develop a model involving teaching assistants as partners to ensure sustainability of the intervention in the school system after the research was completed. This approach builds on a history of large-scale intervention studies conducted at the *Centre for Reading and Language* that have successfully addressed both theoretical and practical concerns (Hatcher, Hulme and Ellis, 1994; Hatcher, Hulme and Snowling, 2004; Hatcher *et al.*, 2006; Bowyer-Crane *et al.*, 2008).

This chapter offers an overview of the York Reading for Meaning Project. This large-scale project was a randomised controlled trial (RCT) carried out with 20 primary schools in the north of England, to evaluate three intervention programmes designed to support reading comprehension. The scientific report of this project (Clarke, Snowling, Truelove and Hulme, 2010) was published in *Psychological Science*. Shorter summaries of the

Developing Reading Comprehension, First Edition. Paula J. Clarke, Emma Truelove, Charles Hulme and Margaret J. Snowling.
© 2014 John Wiley & Sons, Ltd. Published 2014 by John Wiley & Sons, Ltd.

project can be found in a practitioner review (Duff and Clarke, 2011), in a book chapter (Clarke, Henderson and Truelove, 2010) and on the project's webpage (www.readingformeaning.co.uk). This chapter outlines the aims, design, assessments and findings of the project.

THEORETICAL AIMS

The Reading for Meaning Project set out to test some simple hypotheses about the cognitive factors that may cause problems in developing adequate reading comprehension. Intervention studies provide powerful ways of testing hypotheses about the cognitive causes of a learning difficulty. We wanted to test two different ideas. The first was that the causes of poor reading comprehension lie in the metacognitive processes that contribute to text-level comprehension – namely the strategies that are used to ensure text cohesion and understanding. The second was that the causes of poor reading comprehension are in the oral language processes that underpin comprehension. Accordingly we designed a Text Level and an Oral Language Intervention Programme and compared the progress of children receiving each of these with that of an untaught control group. In addition a third group received an integrated intervention programme involving both Oral Language intervention and Text Level training.

At the text level, a number of studies have taught specific strategies for working with text that benefit poor comprehenders (e.g. Yuill and Oakhill, 1988; Oakhill and Patel, 1991). We aimed to replicate and extend this work by combining a number of different text-based strategies, such as mental imagery, within the Text Comprehension intervention package.

Considering the widely documented oral language difficulties of children with weaknesses in reading comprehension discussed in Chapter 2, we found it surprising that little attention had been paid to supporting language skills as a means of improving reading comprehension. We wanted to redress this balance and investigate the idea that by improving oral language skills we could also improve reading comprehension in poor comprehenders. Finally, given the close links between oral and written language processes, we wanted to investigate whether an integrated programme of activities to support language skills in both domains would maximise gains in reading comprehension. Figure 3.1 provides an overview of the three interventions evaluated in this study.

As mentioned in the opening of this chapter, we felt it important to address the complexity of reading comprehension processes by developing interventions with several components that have an evidence base for supporting reading comprehension. As a result we developed 'multicomponential' packages of intervention, which included the following components:

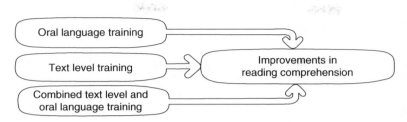

Figure 3.1   A summary of the three intervention approaches investigated in the Reading for Meaning Project

Oral Language Programme: vocabulary, reciprocal teaching with spoken language, figurative language and spoken narrative

Text Level Programme: metacognitive strategies, reciprocal teaching with written language, inferencing from text and written narrative

Combined Programme: all of the above (vocabulary, reciprocal teaching with spoken language, figurative language, spoken narrative, metacognitive strategies, reciprocal teaching with written language, inferencing from text and written narrative)

It is important to acknowledge that there are benefits and drawbacks of a multicomponential approach. On the plus side, the variety of components and activities maximise the chances of it being effective with the greatest number of children. This 'something for everyone' style of intervention is less risky than an approach based on a single strategy. A multicomponential approach is therefore more likely to include a teaching approach, which will support a given child and hence could be considered more ethical. This is an important consideration because there are different reasons why children might develop the poor comprehender profile and there is a variation among them in both cognitive profile and learning styles.

A drawback of the multicomponent approach, however, is that it is difficult to disentangle specific effects. If children make significant gains on a reading test as a result of receiving one of the programmes, then the question which inevitably follows is: which aspect of the training caused the improvement? To attempt to unravel this issue, it is necessary to have assessments that tap into each of the components taught. Using statistical techniques (which will be described in more depth later in this chapter), it is then possible to examine whether improvements in a certain component can predict improvements in reading gains. This method relies on having reliable, valid tests that are closely aligned with the component skills. Selection and creation of such measures can be challenging and, furthermore, some aspects of reading comprehension are difficult to measure objectively.

PRACTICAL AIMS

Following an extensive search of the literature and informed by discussions with a liaison group (comprising educational psychologists, speech and language therapists, specialist teachers and other professionals) our research team decided that the most appropriate form of intervention was a stand-alone programme of additional support beyond regular classroom activity. In order to complement work in the classroom, we recognised that the intervention should be compatible with the learning objectives of the Primary National Strategy (Department for Education and Skills, Primary Framework for Literacy and Mathematics, 2006), which represented government guidance at the time. An important practical aim was therefore to ensure that components in the intervention linked to the objectives of the primary framework for literacy, in particular 'understanding and interpreting texts; engaging and responding to texts; and text structure and organisation'.

Our key practical focus was the involvement of teaching assistants as partners in developing and delivering the interventions. As discussed by Carroll *et al*. (2011), the role of teaching assistants in intervention and specialist support for children with Special Educational Needs has increased over recent years. Like those authors, we strongly support this practice and our project aimed to equip teaching assistants with the skills and materials required to deliver high quality intervention. Our research was, to our knowledge, the first project to require teaching assistants to deliver three different packages of intervention in parallel. Recognising that this was a challenge, we wanted to investigate the experiences of teaching assistants during the process and to reflect on this we have included the insights of two teaching assistants at relevant points in this book. Given the complexity of delivering multiple components within single sessions, we felt it was important to give teaching assistants a foundation of psychological knowledge by introducing them to theories and the evidence base supporting the effectiveness of different approaches. Our aim was to produce a 'manualised' intervention with in-built flexibility that would allow the teaching assistants to use programme flexibility in response to children's individual abilities and needs.

INTERVENTION DESIGN

This section will outline the general features of the intervention programmes. Details of their contents are provided in Chapters 5, 6 and 7 and an overview of the teaching principles underlying the intervention activities is given in Chapter 4.

One of the initial decisions to be made was what the overall length of the intervention programmes should be. Previous research had demonstrated impressive gains in reading comprehension skills over relatively short time periods (e.g. Oakhill and Patel, 1991 – three 20-minute sessions; Johnson-Glenberg, 2001 – 28 30-minute sessions in a 10-week period; Yuill and Oakhill, 1988 – six 45-minute sessions); we were hopeful that it would be possible to replicate such progress. A previous intervention study by our group (Bowyer-Crane et al., 2008) had been run over a period of 20 weeks and our liaison group felt this length was feasible and appropriate for the current study. To allow children the opportunity to consolidate their learning, we considered it necessary to have frequent sessions; therefore three sessions per week were included, two of which were delivered to pairs of children and one was individual. The sessions were designed to be delivered in a fixed order, with paired sessions scheduled at the start and middle of each week and the individual sessions taking place at the end.

In total, the programmes were 60 sessions long and these were divided into two 10-week blocks. The decision to have distinct teaching blocks was largely driven by the school timetable and the need to schedule assessment time periods around school holidays. Furthermore, the precise scheduling of the sessions was not fixed, allowing schools flexibility to work around their existing timetable. Most schools opted to run sessions at times outside of literacy lessons to ensure that the intervention was supplementary to classroom teaching. In some schools, sessions occurred before school and in others session times were rotated to ensure that children did not routinely miss the same lessons.

The overall form of the intervention programmes was carefully planned to ensure a wide coverage of reading material and component skills. We considered it important to reflect the diverse range of reading material that children encounter in school and so a variety of fiction, non-fiction and poetry was selected, adapted and written for the purposes of the study. We were mindful of the importance of including material with wide-ranging appeal to children with different preferences and interests. Selection was also informed by the liaison group, teaching assistants and published book lists available online.

A distinctive feature of the intervention design was the inclusion of multiple components in each session. This design follows the principles of 'distributed practice', which asserts the effectiveness of 'little and often' teaching of new skills. The components were therefore bite-sized learning experiences that built over time through repetitive structure and instruction. Routine components were included within 30-minute sessions and taught through varied activities integrated around a theme or text. Thirty minutes was considered to be the optimum length for teaching,

Oral Language programme

Approx. time	3 mins	5 mins	7 mins	5 mins	7 mins	3 mins
Activity	Introduction	Vocabulary	Reciprocal teaching with spoken language	Figurative language	Spoken narrative	Plenary

Figure 3.2 Components and session structures used in the Oral Language intervention programmes

Text Level programme

Approx. time	3 mins	5 mins	7 mins	5 mins	7 mins	3 mins
Activity	Introduction	Metacognative strategies	Reciprocal teaching with written language	Inferencing from text	Written narrative	Plenary

Figure 3.3 Components and session structures used in the Text Level intervention programmes

taking into account concentration levels, time to cover material and time to settle and summarise. Strategies were introduced gradually and built over time and the programme included immediate, mid- and long-term objectives and outputs.

The components included in each programme are highlighted in Figures 3.2 and 3.3.

Common to both the Oral Language and Text Level programmes is a six-part structure to each session. The first and last sections were included to provide an opportunity for introduction, recapping and consolidation. Teaching Assistants were provided with general prompts to facilitate these introductory and plenary sections but were also encouraged to tailor the interaction to individual children's needs. The intervening sections comprised the main teaching activities. As can be seen in Figures 3.2 and 3.3, the Oral Language and Text Level programmes contained four routine components that were taught in small chunks lasting 5 or 7 minutes within every session. The order of the components in each session was fixed and provided a familiar sequence of taught material. This design feature was deliberate as we wanted children to quickly become accustomed to the session structure and the expectations that would be placed on them. We hoped that the familiar structure would maximise engagement with the activities. Slightly more time was allowed for the reciprocal teaching components as it was at this point in the session that a 'text for the day' was typically introduced. Also, extra time was allocated to the narrative component because this component usually involved substantial output (e.g. written or recorded story generation).

Devising the Combined programme was more challenging. From a research perspective, we wanted to ensure that all Oral Language and

COM programme – variant 1

Approx. time	2.5 mins	5 mins	5 mins	5 mins	5 mins	5 mins	2.5 mins
Activity	Introduction	Metacognative strategies	Reciprocal teaching with written language	Reciprocal teaching with spoken language	Figurative language	Spoken narrative	Plenary

COM programme – variant 2

Approx. time	2.5 mins	5 mins	5 mins	5 mins	5 mins	5 mins	2.5 mins
Activity	Introduction	Vocabulary	Reciprocal teaching with spoken language	Reciprocal teaching with written language	Inferencing from text	Written narrative	Plenary

Figure 3.4   Two example variants of the components and session structures used in the Combined programme

Text Level components received the same amount of coverage; however, it was not possible to do this using an equivalent six section structure. As a result, the Combined programme was carefully structured with a balance of components across the weeks but not an identical structure in every session. Figure 3.4 shows two example combinations of components in two different sessions (for a full overview of all variants see Chapter 7).

Part of the purpose of the Combined programme was to make explicit links between spoken and written language and therefore it was necessary to include reciprocal teaching activities in response to oral language and text in each session. We hoped that this would prompt recognition that the same strategies could be applied to spoken and written language.

A further consideration in designing the Combined programme sessions was to ensure that components that were complimentary were adjacent within the session structure, for example with vocabulary preceding listening comprehension and reading comprehension preceding inferencing from text. One concession was the reduced time allocated to each section. Therefore the children who received the Combined programme experienced all components but at half the quantity of the other two intervention programmes.

RESEARCH DESIGN

Understanding Causality

As mentioned above, a key motivation for conducting an intervention study is to investigate theories about the causes of children's learning difficulties. Much educational research is interested in establishing cause and effect. To be able to understand the development of children's learning, it is crucial to identify and understand drivers of change. An intervention aims to facilitate change in a particular skill (e.g. reading comprehension) and evaluate the extent to which change has occurred. In order to be confident that what has been put in place has caused the change, one needs to be able to rule out all other possible explanations.

A practical example of this would be a teacher who is keen to effect a change in pupils' mathematical reasoning skills. The teacher has read about two possible techniques for improving those skills and is keen to evaluate which is the most successful. The teacher chooses to use one technique with one class of pupils (method A) and another technique with another class (method B). Following a period of teaching, the pupils' mathematical reasoning is assessed. The teacher discovers that pupils who have received method A achieved significantly higher scores than those who had been taught using method B. This finding immediately raises the question 'were the higher scores due to the use of teaching method A? (see the summary in Figure 3.5).

In order to conclude that this is the case, the teacher needs to establish that there is no other explanation for the improvement. This conclusion is open to doubt as there are many other factors that may have played a role in the differences in outcomes for the two classes. For example, the pupils' starting levels in maths may have differed and those taught with method A

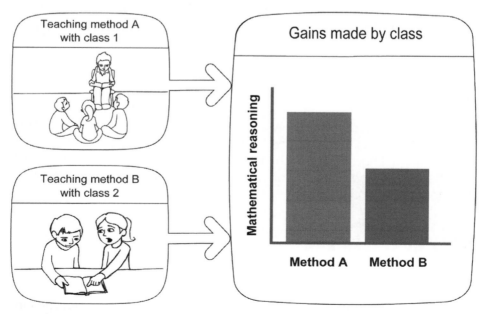

Figure 3.5 A hypothetical scenario to illustrate a basic intervention procedure

may have had stronger skills to begin with. Furthermore, the attendance of pupils in method B may have been poorer, resulting in children receiving less teaching. In addition, the mathematical reasoning test may have been more aligned with the skills taught in method A than those in method B. As you are reading this, you will no doubt think of many more possibilities!

Randomised Controlled Trials

A randomised controlled trial (RCT) design minimises the possible impact of uncontrolled or unknown factors affecting the progress of participants receiving a 'treatment'. In a randomised study people who are eligible for a 'treatment' are assigned 'at random' to either receive an intervention or to be in a control group. The point about random assignment is that it controls for unmeasured differences between people in the groups – using random assignment makes the existence of pre-existing differences between groups very unlikely as an explanation for differences in outcome. The simplest design is where the control group receive no treatment though sometimes (as in the *Reading for Meaning Project*) they receive the treatment later (after the first group have completed the intervention). An excellent overview of the details of RCT methods and how to conduct them is given in David and Carole Torgerson's (2008) book *Designing and Running Randomised Trials in Health Education and the Social Sciences* (see also Carroll *et al.*, 2011).

Sample Considerations

An important consideration in an RCT is the sample of children receiving the intervention. In the example above, without knowing more about the characteristics of the pupils and the schools, it is difficult to predict whether similar results would be obtained in another school. Therefore it is of prime importance to employ criteria for inclusion and collect baseline data about the profile of the sample. In the *York Reading for Meaning Project*, we invited a large number of schools across a wide geographical region to take part and collected information about the characteristics of the sample, including their performance on standardised tests and their socio-economic status. This allowed us to judge how representative our sample was and the extent to which the findings should generalise to other schools and pupils.

Random Allocation

One of the core features of an RCT is random allocation of children to treatments. Consider the example described earlier – if the pupils had been randomly assigned to method A or method B then any differences between the groups in terms of starting levels would be distributed by chance across the two teaching methods. With a large enough number of children in each group, it is likely that the starting levels would be approximately equal between the two teaching methods, effectively ruling out different starting levels as an explanation of the higher scores for group A at the end of the intervention. In educational settings, the process of random allocation may run counter to a teacher's instincts regarding children's needs, behaviours and preferred learning styles. As a result, random allocation can create a tension at the point of revealing the allocated groups to school staff. Nevertheless, random allocation is a necessary part of the research design we chose.

In the case of the *York Reading for Meaning Project*, we were confident that random allocation was appropriate and ethical because there was sufficient evidence to suggest that all of the approaches had potential benefit (and the waiting list control group would also receive help). Randomisation took place within schools, resulting in children being randomly allocated to the three intervention groups (Oral Language, Text Level and Combined) and the waiting control group (further details about the waiting control group can be found in later sections of this chapter) within each school. All interventions were delivered by the same teaching assistant (TA) in each school. The reason this is important is clear from the example above: if method A had been delivered by one teacher and method B by another, it would not be possible to disentangle the effects of the teaching method from the teaching styles and personalities of the teachers. What is more, by implementing all interventions in all schools, we were also able to control for possible school effects. Referring back to the example, if method A had been trialled in one school and method B trialled in another school, the influence of school factors (such as class size, school values and geographical area) may influence the results obtained. Therefore, it was important to ensure that all three intervention programmes ran in each school so that we could be confident that any differences were due to the interventions and not a feature of particular schools.

Blinding

Another key feature of the design we used is 'blinding'. In the example above, it is possible that the teacher, when giving the test, may have inadvertently or subconsciously biased performance, for example by offering more time or encouragement to those in one group over the other. Blinding requires that those assessing change are unaware of the interventions that have been received and consequently are unable to introduce any systematic bias.

Attendance and Attrition

Ideally, to evaluate the effectiveness of different interventions, all pupils should receive the full programmes. This, however, is not always feasible and inevitably students will miss sessions for a variety of reasons. In some cases children may move schools and therefore leave the trial before it is completed (this is known as 'attrition'). The RCT protocol requires that attendance and attrition to be reported carefully. In terms of our example, if the class who had received method A had 90% attendance and the class who had received method B had 75% attendance, then the higher score could simply reflect the amount of teaching received. Furthermore, if the class taught using method A lost 5 pupils during the term compared to the method B class who lost 1 pupil, then a number of factors introduced by this attrition must be considered when interpreting the results. The basic issue here is that if attrition does not occur randomly it can bias the outcome of a trial. Suppose, for example, that the children with the greatest difficulties were more likely to drop out of one group – this will artificially 'inflate' the scores obtained by that group at the end of the trial (the children expected to get the lowest scores will not be tested because they have withdrawn). In the present study, we followed the CONSORT guidance (http://www.consort-statement.org/, last accessed 08/2012) and where possible sought to continue working with children who moved schools. Furthermore, we carefully documented attendance and any significant events affecting intervention delivery and completion.

Control Groups

A final feature of the intervention research design we used is to include comparison with peers who continue to receive normal classroom teaching. In intervention studies, the employment of a control group is important as it allows us to rule out the possibility that gains would have been made regardless of whether or not a specific intervention had been implemented. In our example, it would have been advisable to compare the test results of teaching method A and B with those from another group who continued to receive teaching using standard techniques. It could have been that this group made similar gains to those in method A and if this were the case we could not conclude that teaching method A was effective.

In the *York Reading for Meaning Project*, we used a waiting list control group. The children in this group were selected, allocated and monitored in exactly the same way as those in the intervention groups; however, whilst the other three groups received intervention, children in the waiting list control group continued with normal classroom activities. This aspect of the design was important on ethical grounds to ensure that the children in the waiting control group received intervention, given that their needs had been highlighted through the process of selection; however, crucially, the intervention was only implemented *after* the final assessment point to allow us to compare the three intervention groups to normal classroom practice. The decision to use a waiting list control group was considered appropriate as the intervention programmes were created to be applicable to children across Key Stage 2. Furthermore, we did not consider it detrimental to children's development to receive the intervention at a later date. Clearly, in other circumstances a waiting control design may not be appropriate or ethically justifiable.

Establishing Long-Term Educational Significance

Of prime importance to educators is the extent to which interventions can benefit children in the long term. It is noticeable that many published intervention studies only report gains immediately after intervention (e.g. Johnson-Glenberg, 2000). Furthermore, where studies do include a maintenance assessment, the time lag between completing the intervention and testing is often short (e.g. 6 weeks after the intervention in a study by Biemiller and Boote, 2006). To address these limitations, the present study used an 11-month maintenance period after the interventions were complete, during which all groups received typical classroom instruction. Following this delay, performance on reading comprehension measures was reassessed to find out whether improvements had been sustained. See Figure 3.6 for the timeline of the project.

As many of the intervention activities focused on strategy-based learning, we wanted to examine whether strategy use generalised to novel learning contexts. This 11-month period provided a window in which children could practise and fine-tune these new approaches as they became

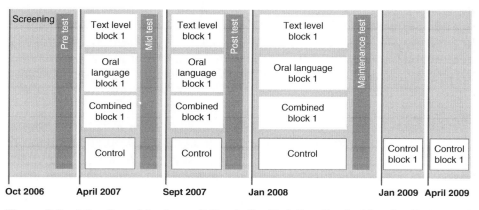

Figure 3.6 A timeline of the key activities in the *York Reading for Meaning Project*

more independent learners. Furthermore, recognising that reading com-prehension skills are of paramount importance across the curriculum, this period opened up opportunities for consolidating strategies in multi-ple contexts and different subject areas.

The follow-up assessment enabled us to assess the impact of the three different intervention programmes in the longer term and to ask questions about the predictors of individual differences in progress.

From a practical perspective, it is vital to be able to demonstrate the dura-bility and generalisability of gains if an intervention is to be implemented on a larger scale once a research study is completed. For ethical reasons, educators need to be confident that any programmes that require with-drawal from regular classroom activities will result in long-term benefits above and beyond those that would have been possible in the classroom. Furthermore, in order to make judgements regarding value for money, schools need evidence of the size and durability of expected gains.

Control Task

When children receive additional or different support, particularly in a small group or 1:1 context, it could be anticipated that they will show a general boost in performance. This boost (sometimes referred to as a Hawthorne effect) may be due to a variety of factors, such as increased motivation, concentration and focus. To be able to disentangle the effects of these factors from those of the intervention methods, it is essential to monitor performance on measures that are unrelated to the intervention activities. In the case of the present study, arithmetic was chosen as a control meas-ure because we did not predict that oral language or text-level work would improve basic numerical skills. Should we find that children improve not only on measures of reading comprehension but also on the control task, it would not be possible to conclude that the intervention has specific effects.

Figure 3.7 summarises the key principles and recommendations to consider when designing, evaluating and reporting interventions.

ASSESSMENT

The children with reading comprehension impairment who took part in the *Reading for Meaning Project* were identified following screening of approximately 1000 children in 20 Year 4 classes. The tests included in the screening phase were chosen to enable us to identify children whose general cognitive ability was within the normal range and who demonstrated age-appropriate decoding skills alongside relatively weak comprehension skills. For ease of administration, three group

Participants

- Studies should report whether the sample has been self-selected, referred, randomly selected etc. as this may affect the validity of the findings.

- If children with specific learning profiles are included then selection should be made using established criteria and should be based on performance measured using standardised tests.

- Criteria for inclusion in the study should be clearly stated so that the findings can be applied appropriately.

- Studies should conduct statistical power calculations to demonstrate that their sample size is sufficient. They should also report the dropout rate of individuals and the number of individuals who completed assessments.

- Samples often contain a large amount of variation. In order to make conclusions about the generalisability of findings, studies must acknowledge the extent to which the participants are comparable to other groups of participants selected in the same way.

Design

- If a control group has not been used then the conclusions that can be made from the study are limited. An intervention may lead to improvements in a particular skill but it is important to know whether those improvements would have occurred anyway as part of natural development or regular schooling.

- Selection criteria for the control group will depend on the purpose of the study. If a study is trying to demonstrate the effectiveness of a particular teaching approach then an untreated or waiting control group will give the strongest evidence. If a study is attempting to control for factors such as withdrawal from class, impact of additional 1:1 or group support, then it may be beneficial to use a treated control group who complete an intervention which is unrelated in content to the intervention being trialled.

- The strongest evidence comes from studies which have randomly allocated participants from the same sample to intervention and control groups. Randomisation attempts to control for the effects of additional factors that are beyond the control of the researcher. Large sample sizes are required for randomisation to be effective. Additional factors should be equally distributed in groups that have been formed through randomisation; their influence should therefore be the same in each group, and should not distort the effects of intervention.

Intervention

- If a study aims to address the issue of causality then it is imperative that the intervention is described in detail so that interpretations can be made about what may be driving changes in performance.

- The origins of intervention approaches and content should be acknowledged. How they link to theory and previous evidence of efficacy should be demonstrated.

- The delivery method should be fully explained to allow practitioners to evaluate feasibility of implementation in education contexts. Delivery factors (e.g. computerised, tutor led, small group, individual) may also be important in interpreting the results of the study.

- To increase confidence in the study's findings, it is important that there has been an attempt to monitor the extent to which the intervention has been delivered as intended. Such measures may include observations and manualised instructions.

Figure 3.7 Key principles and recommendations for the design, evaluation and reporting interventions (after Duff and Clarke, 2011)

Measures

• From the outset, a study should have clearly identified primary and secondary outcome measures. These should remain the same throughout the study. The effectiveness of a study should be judged largely on its primary outcome measures.

• There are clear benefits of using a combination of bespoke and standardised tests. Bespoke tests allow the researcher to address whether specific components of interventions have been effective whereas standardised tests give an indication of the generalisability of the findings. If a study uses bespoke measures only, then it needs to clarify the extent to which the bespoke measure is similar to the content of the teaching sessions; it is possible that in some cases interventions may be teaching to the test.

• Blind assessment reduces the possibility of the assessor introducing bias to the data. Ideally assessments should be carried out by individuals who are independent and unaware of the aims of the research so that they can be as objective as possible.

Results

• Measures of central tendency (e.g. mean) and variation (e.g. standard deviation) should be reported so that the reader can ascertain both group level performance and individual variability. If there is substantial variability within groups then the likelihood of a statistically significant difference between groups is reduced.

• There should be sufficient details about the nature of the data reported for the reader to be able to evaluate whether the statistical methods employed are appropriate.

• If there are data missing then the authors should provide an explanation as to why. It is important that the number of data points being included in each mean are reported as it may differ from the original sample size, due to drop out of participants.

• Full statistical output is required to be able to examine whether the analyses have been conducted correctly, and to evaluate the size of group differences and intervention effects. Authors should not be selective in what they report; both null and significant findings should be acknowledged.

Conclusions

• If a control group has been used then conclusions must be based on the extent to which improvements made by the treatment group differ from those of the controls.

• Conclusions should be traced back to the data and the results of statistical analyses. They should be clearly specified and unambiguous. The study's take home message should not be open to misinterpretation.

• The conclusions should reflect the aims of the study and be independent of personal, political and commercial agendas.

Figure 3.7 (*continued*)

administered tests were selected: a test of spelling (since spelling skills correlate strongly with word decoding skills), a test of listening comprehension (as a proxy for reading comprehension) and a non-verbal reasoning test (Matrices; see Raven, 1998) to provide an estimate of general cognitive abilities. In each school the children who achieved the lowest scores on the listening comprehension task relative to their peers were identified. Of these, those with age-appropriate spelling and non-verbal ability in the normal range (standard score of above 85) were selected for individual assessment.

The tests, which we administered individually, were selected to provide a valid and reliable assessment of word-level decoding and reading comprehension since we wanted to identify children with well-developed reading accuracy and fluency but difficulties in understanding what they read. The tests chosen were the *Test of Word Reading Efficiency* (TOWRE) (Torgesen, Wagner and Rashotte, 1997), which requires children to read aloud as quickly and accurately as possible a list of words and of non-words (and takes approximately two minutes to complete), and the *Neale Analysis of Reading Ability* (NARA II) (Neale, 1989), which requires children to read passages and then answer questions about them.

In each school we next ranked the children according to the magnitude of the discrepancy in standard score points between their attainments on the NARA II reading comprehension and TOWRE word reading efficiency tests; finally, the eight children with the greatest discrepancies within the subsample tested from their year group were chosen as suitable candidates for the intervention. The children within each school were then allocated randomly to one of four groups, three groups of two children were to receive each of the interventions and another group of two children were allocated to the waiting list control group.

In order to evaluate the efficacy of the three interventions, it was necessary to monitor the progress of the children in the intervention closely as well as that of their peers in the waiting control group. To do this we assessed all of the children just before the intervention began (Time 1), 10 weeks later at mid test (Time 2), 10 weeks later at the end of the intervention (Time 3) and, finally, following a period of 11 months to investigate maintenance of gains (Time 4). The primary outcome measures were tests of reading comprehension, namely the NARA II and the Wechsler Individual Achievement Test (WIAT-II) (Wechsler, 2005) Reading Comprehension subtest. The WIAT-II is an individually administered test consisting of a range of different reading materials including sentences, passages and reviews, non-fiction and fiction. Children are asked open-ended comprehension questions tapping literal, inferential and vocabulary-dependent understanding, prediction, summarisation and question generation. Secondary outcomes were assessed using a range of measures tapping specific abilities targeted in the intervention programmes, including listening comprehension, vocabulary and figurative language, and, as mentioned above, a test of basic arithmetic was included as a control task. Additional tests were given at different time points but will not be discussed here (see Clarke, Snowling, Truelove and Hulme, 2010, for details).

FINDINGS

The progress made by the children in the three intervention groups as a result of the interventions was encouraging when compared with progress made by the waiting list control group who received normal classroom input. Figure 3.8 shows the gains made on the WIAT Reading Comprehension subtest by the children in the three intervention conditions, compared with the progress made by those in the waiting list control group. Gains are shown in standard score points, a metric based on population norms. In each case, the gain is the score achieved after the intervention when baseline performance is taken into account. The data were analysed using a statistical technique that takes into account differences in performance at Time 1 before the intervention began; it also controls for the fact that children were clustered within schools (receiving intervention from the same TA) since this could have made a difference.

As shown in Figure 3.8, all three interventions brought about gains in text comprehension after 20 weeks of training, as measured by the WIAT-II Reading Comprehension subtest. The average gain was 3 standard score points, which is small but statistically significant. The figure also shows the scores of the children at follow-up 11 months later. All of the gains remained significant but, strikingly, the performance of the children in the Oral Language intervention was now significantly ahead of that of the children who received the Text Level and Combined programmes. The children in this group had made an average gain of 7 standard score points more than controls, progress that can be considered not only statistically but also educationally significant.

Gains on the NARA II were less impressive. For this measure, the gains made by the Intervention groups were not statistically different to those

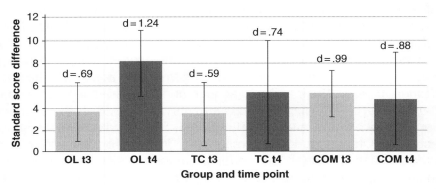

Figure 3.8 The gains made by each intervention group relative to the control group on the WIAT Reading Comprehension subtest

made by the control group, who also improved (perhaps because of practice effects). Turning to the other measures: importantly, the Oral Language intervention group significantly outperformed the control group on a standardised measure of vocabulary (WASI; Wechsler, 1999) requiring words to be defined orally, and both the Oral Language and Combined groups (but not the Text Level or control groups) showed improved knowledge of vocabulary and idioms. For the WIAT-II Numerical Operations test (a measure of arithmetic skills), at Time 3 there were small and similar-sized improvements in all three intervention groups compared with the control group. The advantage of the Combined group was just significantly better than the control group at Time 3 (while neither of the other groups were statistically better than the control group). However, these effects had dissipated by Time 4 (11 months after the intervention had finished). In short, it seems that the effect of the interventions on reading comprehension at Time 4 were selective and cannot be explained as a general effect that operates to bring about improvements on skills that have not been directly taught.

The study design used here did not permit a clear answer to the important question of which components of the different interventions caused the gains in reading comprehension. However, two of the interventions (the Oral Language and Combined) brought about gains in vocabulary; this allowed us to test the hypothesis that growth in vocabulary might be one cause of improvements in comprehension skill. We did this using a statistical method called 'mediation' analysis. Such an analysis asks the question 'are the gains in reading comprehension proportional to (mediated by) improvements in vocabulary?' The measure of vocabulary used was from Time 3 and based on children's ability to provide oral definitions to words they had been taught in the intervention (as well as untaught words); we assessed whether this predicted reading comprehension outcomes at Time 4.

Our findings revealed that gains in reading comprehension scores at Time 4 were partially mediated by gains in vocabulary for children in the Oral Language intervention group – but other skills also contributed to the progress they made. However, for children who received the Combined programme, their comprehension gains were entirely due to growth in vocabulary. Thus, findings strongly suggest that one aspect of children's oral language skills (their ability to acquire and express vocabulary knowledge) is one cause of the improvements in reading comprehension observed in two of the interventions studied. This, coupled with the strong effect of the Oral Language programme at Time 4, provides evidence for the theory that difficulties with reading comprehension frequently arise from oral language comprehension difficulties (including, but not restricted to, limitations of vocabulary knowledge).

In summary, the *York Reading for Meaning Project* showed that, for children who reach middle school age and have specific difficulties with reading comprehension, a number of different approaches are effective. The children in the project benefited from a systematic intervention programme delivered through the written modality, incorporating activities to improve text comprehension strategies, inferencing skills and the understanding of story structure and narrative. However, a novel finding of our research was that similar gains were made after following an Oral Language intervention that focused on promoting listening comprehension, vocabulary, figurative language and oral narrative skills, and there were equivalent benefits of combining the two approaches.

Importantly, in terms of sustained benefits, our results revealed that the Oral Language approach was the most effective in that the children who received this programme continued to forge ahead after the intervention ceased. Whilst arguably counter-intuitive, these findings are what might be expected if the proximal cause of reading comprehension impairments is oral language difficulties. This is a clear example of testing a causal hypothesis; the Oral Language programme was theoretically motivated not only by the Simple Model of Reading (Gough and Tunmer, 1986; see Chapter 1) but also by our understanding of the specific difficulties of those who show the poor comprehender profile. The fact that the Oral Language programme was found to be effective, and its positive effects were mediated by gains in vocabulary, provides support for the hypothesis that reading comprehension difficulties arise (at least in part) from underlying difficulties in comprehending spoken language.

It is important to consider what caused the sustained effects of the Oral Language programme on reading comprehension after the end of the intervention. A simple explanation might be that growth in vocabulary increases an individual's ability to understand not only single words but also sentences and arguably increases resources that are available for making inferences across the text. An alternative view might be that children who receive oral language training become somehow more engaged with learning and this accounts for the further gains that they made.

SUMMARY AND CONCLUSIONS

The findings from the *York Reading for Meaning Project* have a number of theoretical and practical implications. On a practical level, it is important to note that all three interventions (Text Level, Oral Language and Combined) improved children's reading comprehension skills. However, it is notable that at the delayed test (11 months after the intervention had finished), the advantage of the Oral Language group on the WIAT Reading Comprehension test had increased in comparison to the other two groups. This selective increase is an important effect and suggests that the Oral Language intervention programme had brought about some durable changes in language and reading comprehension skills, which actually grew stronger after the intervention had finished. This suggests that the Oral Language intervention overall was the most effective of the three programmes. Theoretically, this finding provides strong support for the theory that the reading comprehension difficulties seen in those who show the poor comprehender profile are a secondary consequence of these children's oral language weaknesses. This conclusion is also consistent with the important role played by increases in vocabulary knowledge as a mediator of the effects of the Oral Language and Combined interventions.

APPENDICES

The appendices for this chapter (included at the end of the book) provide details of the processes involved in the actual running of the *York Reading for Meaning Project*. The day-to-day activities were managed by the research team with support from Elizabeth Fieldsend, an educational consultant with extensive experience of teaching and advising in schools. Many of the approaches used in the management of the project were informed by the research team's experiences of earlier intervention projects (Hatcher, Hulme and Ellis, 1994; Hatcher, Hulme and Snowling, 2004; Hatcher *et al.*, 2006; Bowyer-Crane *et al.*, 2008). These appendices provide insight into the planning, organisation and administration that goes into an education-based RCT; they should therefore be useful and of interest to those wishing to conduct similar trials, those involved in training and supporting teaching assistants, and practitioners and researchers working together in partnership.

Chapter 4

Teaching Principles

This chapter provides an overview of the three intervention programmes that we developed for the York Reading for Meaning Project. We begin by considering the core principles underpinning the intervention programmes. We spent a considerable amount of time discussing these with the teaching assistants in order to prepare them to implement the interventions. In order to underline their importance, we returned to them frequently when supporting delivery of the programmes.

VYGOTSKIAN PRINCIPLES

Vygotsky (1962, 1978) is widely known for the socio-cultural theory of learning, which places emphasis on the importance of social interaction for the development of cognitive skills. This theory has been highly influential in educational practice (see Göncü and Gauvain, 2011, for a recent review) and provides the rationale for some of the features of the intervention programmes developed for this project. Vygotsky viewed learning as being socially mediated and argued that knowledge is constructed by people together, in social situations. He highlighted the importance of language as a tool in social interaction and learning and argued that language is influential in transforming thinking. These ideas are consistent with the learning environments that we set up in this project. Children and tutors collaborated on activities and exchanged ideas and perspectives through spoken and written language. Every effort was made to ensure that the sessions were rich social interactions and teaching assistants were provided with extensive scripts and prompts to guide interactions and maximise learning opportunities.

Developing Reading Comprehension, First Edition. Paula J. Clarke, Emma Truelove,
Charles Hulme and Margaret J. Snowling.
© 2014 John Wiley & Sons, Ltd. Published 2014 by John Wiley & Sons, Ltd.

Peer Learning

An important feature of the learning contexts set up for this project was the opportunity for peer collaboration. Cooperative learning, in which peers listen to one another's ideas about text and support one another to use strategies, was highlighted as one of the most effective methods for improving reading comprehension by the National Reading Panel (2000). Cooperative learning was embedded into the current intervention programmes. All programmes followed the same structure, with each having three sessions per week. As previously outlined, the first two sessions were delivered as paired sessions and the third as an individual session. The paired sessions were included to provide extensive opportunity for children to engage in discussions with their teaching assistant and, importantly, in line with the principles of cooperative learning, with each other. Teaching assistants reported considerable variation across the pairs. This was an inevitable consequence of the random allocation process used. Since the pairing of children was random, some children worked with a peer of the same gender and others did not; some children were working with friends whilst others were paired with children they knew less well. A further point was that, although broadly speaking the children in the study had similar profiles (reading accuracy stronger than reading comprehension), there was variation between children in terms of their attainment and comprehension skill. These differences resulted in some pairings being closely matched in terms of

Box 4.1   TA commentary

I was interested to see how the random pairings of the children I was assigned to teach would work out. I had two mixed pairings and one all-girl pairing. The abilities of all were very varied and one of the girls in the pairing spoke English as an additional language. I was surprised how it panned out. The girls got on famously straight away. Despite my concern over a large gulf in reading ability of one mixed pair, one didn't hold the other back. The other mixed pair began by wanting to sit at opposite ends of the same table but within a short time were helping, supporting and praising each other, demonstrating a good working partnership.

ability and others being less so. The factors that we have highlighted here are potentially important and certainly warrant further investigation. However, to investigate systematically the issue of 'what comprises an optimal pairing' would require a very large study and was beyond the scope of the current project.

We believe that discussing and sharing ideas and perspectives with a teaching assistant and peer benefits reading comprehension skills in a number of different ways. First, through listening to another's interpretation of a passage, children gain new ideas about its meaning. What is more, children's personal ideas and interpretations can be built upon, revised and questioned in the light of other people's views. These opportunities served to reinforce the message that understanding text is subjective and that words, sentences and passages can be processed and understood differently. By discussing a range of views, it is possible to achieve a collective understanding of the passage that is richer than a single interpretation.

A further benefit of peer learning is the experience of explaining one's own thoughts and views to others. Paired sessions provided a supportive and encouraging space for children to express themselves and practise vocalising their thoughts. Sharing knowledge and ideas in this way promotes social language and skills such as active listening, turn taking and gauging relevance. The intimacy of the paired session may

Box 4.2 TA commentary

I had one child who was particularly quiet in a classroom situation and even found it hard to open up in the paired sessions at first. However, her partner really supported her and she soon gained confidence in putting her ideas forward.

After relatively few weeks, the class teacher of one of the children receiving the intervention sought me out one break time to tell me how amazing it had been for her to see this child, who had almost never volunteered a comment in class teaching sessions, suddenly finding her voice and increasing in confidence. It was a heart warming moment.

also be less intimidating than a classroom situation for some children. Children who find it difficult to share ideas out loud to a class may be more inclined to express their views within a small group; this was especially true during our intervention because children were able to build rapport with their partner and teaching assistant within a safe space over a number of weeks. This particular feature of the intervention programmes may therefore have been especially important in developing children's confidence.

Individualisation

Vygotsky's (1978) concept of the zone of proximal development influenced the inclusion of a weekly individual session in the intervention programmes. This concept suggests that optimal learning takes place in a space between what is currently comfortably achievable for an individual and what cannot be achieved without another's direct help. Individual assessment is vital for establishing a child's present level of ability; once this is established, it is possible to plan and tailor support effectively within the zone of proximal development. Recognizing the individual differences between children in their preferences, experiences and abilities, we deemed it necessary to have some dedicated time devoted to tailoring the programme to individual children's specific needs.

Throughout the paired sessions the teaching assistants were advised to keep track of individual children's progress in the core components and on each of the tasks in order to identify areas to work on in more depth in individual sessions. These sessions were structured similarly to paired sessions with a comprehensive framework and series of activities to complete; however, we advised teaching assistants to adapt and develop these as necessary, to meet the particular needs of each child.

Box 4.3   TA commentary

The individual sessions allowed some of the more uneven pairings a chance to work at their own speed. I soon found that the individual sessions were more important for a particularly quiet child who really had the chance to gain confidence, which gradually allowed her to take part in the paired sessions more fully.

Scaffolding

Consistent with Vygotsky's zone of proximal development is the concept of scaffolding, which originates from Bruner (1978). Scaffolding is particularly important when introducing new tasks, activities and strategies. Rogoff (1990) suggests that the following elements are involved in scaffolding learning: (1) stimulating interest and learner's motivation for carrying out the activity; (2) providing a model or demonstration of how to complete the activity; (3) breaking the activity down into simplified manageable parts so that learners can experience success; (4) providing regular feedback to help learners reflect on their progress.

As the intervention programmes all contained many new ideas for the children, careful scaffolding was deemed essential. Scaffolding was promoted in three main ways: first, we trained teaching assistants in ways of supporting the introduction of new tasks; second, the intervention manuals included scripted models demonstrating how to support the gradual introduction of new tasks, activities and strategies over the course of a number of sessions; third, the games, resources and worksheets were designed to provide scaffolding, for example choice-making was often supported using pictures, symbols and keywords.

We encouraged teaching assistants to reduce scaffolding as the intervention programmes unfolded and we supported their attempts to do so. We felt it was crucial to increase children's independent learning to ensure the generalisation of new learning into the classroom.

Box 4.4 TA commentary

For children who do not enjoy writing, or are worried about their written answers, the scaffolding within the teaching approach enabled them to discuss the work with myself and their peer instead of having to write anything down. The worksheets only had the minimum amount of written work on them and most could simply be discussed if time was short or if a child found the writing off-putting. This allowed them to gain confidence and feel part of the session without the added pressure of having to produce a lot of written work.

Modelling

Drawing on social learning theories (e.g. Bandura, 1977) that emphasize the importance of observation, we were mindful of the need to ensure sufficient opportunities for children to see the teaching assistants carry out the tasks, activities and strategies themselves. To this end, we provided guidance in the manuals that offered opportunities for demonstration and modelling. Modelling has a number of benefits; it gives children concrete examples to relate to and remember, which may help them to understand the requirements of the tasks. Also experiencing another person carrying out a task may help to build confidence and awareness of different perspectives and abilities. Models were typically given as part of initial scaffolding, although the teaching assistants were advised to repeat and reintroduce models as and when necessary.

Reciprocal Teaching

The reciprocal teaching approach aligns with Vygotskian principles and was included in all sessions across all programmes. Reciprocal teaching is a concept that was introduced by Palinscar and Brown in 1984. The approach is supported by a wealth of evidence, largely from studies conducted in the United States. Traditionally, reciprocal teaching has been applied to supporting the understanding of written text; however, in the York Reading for Meaning Project we applied the approach to the understanding of both spoken and written passages. There are two main features of the reciprocal teaching approach. The first of these is the discussion-based method for interacting with the material to be understood. The approach promotes a rich dialogue between the teaching

Box 4.5   TA commentary

The children soon started to take ownership of the sessions, especially during the second round of intervention. They used the knowledge they had gained during the first 10 weeks to quickly move the sessions forward. Their understanding of how sessions ran enabled them to begin to work with very little support from me.

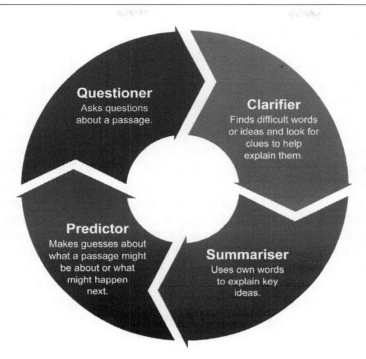

Figure 4.1   The Reciprocal Teaching (Palinscar and Brown, 1984) strategies

assistant and the children in which ideas and responses to the passage are voiced. This discussion is initially led by the teaching assistant, but as the programmes unfold the children themselves take on greater responsibility for leading the dialogue. This reduction of scaffolding over time is a central principle of the Reciprocal Teaching approach and (as mentioned above) was key to our intervention programmes as a means of promoting learner autonomy and generalisation of newly acquired skills to other contexts.

The second main feature of reciprocal teaching is its nature as a strategy-based approach. Four key strategies are targeted, which are clarification, summarisation, prediction and questioning, which are shown in Figure 4.1.

In all programmes the strategies were introduced in this order, that is moving from more straightforward to increasingly complex skills. Once introduced, the strategies were promoted regularly with many opportunities for revision and application built into the sessions. Details of the strategies and how they were implemented in the interventions can be found in the Reciprocal Teaching sections of Chapters 5, 6 and 7.

DISTRIBUTED PRACTICE

The concept of distributed practice was key to the design and implementation of the intervention sessions. Distributed practice can be defined simply as 'a little and often' approach. This was chosen for a number of reasons. First, there is evidence that the distributed practice approach is useful for supporting memory. Seabrook and her colleagues (2005) showed the benefits to memory of distributed practice over massed practice (a lot of practice with few breaks) in education. These researchers compared the two teaching approaches in both laboratory and classroom environments and found that the 'little and often' approach was a more effective method of teaching. Second, we were mindful of the importance of varying the activities within sessions. We recognised that the children taking part were likely to have different preferences for activities. In order to make the sessions as enjoyable as possible we wanted to ensure a range of approaches were included. This meant that if a child was not particularly enjoying one activity they would have a different one to look forward to later in the session. This aspect of the intervention design was regarded as important for ensuring engagement and motivation.

Box 4.6 TA commentary

The variety of activities kept children engaged and they seemed to enjoy the sessions. I never had any child who didn't want to do all the activities in a session, even if they found it difficult at first. The variety of activities and worksheets meant that they didn't have the chance to get bored and the strategies became very familiar in a short space of time.

In our intervention project, activities were repeated regularly in accordance with the principle of distributed practice, giving children many opportunities to revise and revisit the strategies being taught. Children were able to build up their own representations over time and strengthen and develop these as the programmes unfolded. To support recall and recognition of different activities and the demands of these tasks, children were also provided with lots of visual cues. The 'Today we are going to …' poster (Figure 4.2), for example, helped children to monitor their progress

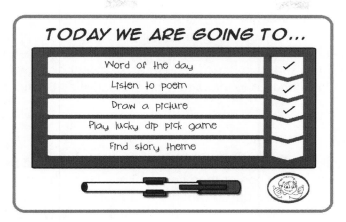

Figure 4.2 The 'Today we are going to …' poster

through the different activities and to understand the sequence of tasks and the structure of sessions. This poster was used differently by different teaching assistants; some chose to fill it in prior to the session and others chose to fill it in with the children at the start of the session.

Box 4.7 TA commentary

I found the poster very helpful for building anticipation at the beginning of the session for what was to follow. Invariably all eyes were on the poster as they greeted me on entering the classroom and they enjoyed taking it in turns to read aloud a point from the poster as I began the introduction to the lesson. This was usually accompanied by excited comments as they found a favourite activity listed.

The extent to which children were able to learn the content and structure of the sessions inevitably varied across the different programmes. Referring back to the structure of the programmes outlined in Chapter 3, the Oral Language and Text Level programmes each contained four teaching components whereas the Combined programme integrated all eight components. This meant that every session in the Oral Language and Text Level programmes covered the same routine components whereas the combination of components varied across Combined sessions. This was unavoidable in this particular research design; however, the number of components taught within a session and the routine structure of components across sessions is something to consider carefully when planning using a distributed practice approach. We intended children to become highly familiar with the expectations of the sessions, hoping that this would reduce any anxiety about what was to come and allow children to focus fully on the activities themselves.

Box 4.8 TA commentary

After only a few sessions I had started to allow the children to fill in parts of the poster themselves. They knew that they were going to read part of a story and have the chance to continue their own stories, so they were able to add these themselves. Gradually we didn't even need the posters as they were predicting the pattern of the sessions so well.

In embedding the distributed practice approach, we were careful to ensure that the sessions did not feel too disjointed. Although each activity was scheduled to last only a few minutes, it was intended that (from the child's perspective) the movement between activities would nonetheless be seamless. This session flow was achieved by having a passage of text at the heart of each session. The focus and emphasis was primarily on the passage and activities, which had been designed to fit into the unfolding discussion of the text. The order of the components was carefully chosen to provide logical journeys through the passages.

Box 4.9 TA commentary

The sessions flowed very well, with the activities being linked closely to the story/text that had been read that session. My children particularly enjoyed listening for the word of the day in the passages.

It is important to note that whilst this was our ideal, it was not always possible to find passages that contained everything that was needed for each activity. It was particularly challenging, for example, to find passages that had clear bridging inferences that could be used as examples in the early stages of supporting this type of inferencing. Therefore in some circumstance more stand-alone activities were necessary. In the case of bridging inferences, worksheets with clear examples were used and once completed the children were then encouraged to use these learning experiences and apply the strategies practised to all passages.

THEMES

Programme content was themed to provide maximum opportunities for making links and for consolidation. The themes were identified through consultation with teachers and education professionals and through careful inspection of the curriculum topics being covered in the UK with children aged eight to ten years. Choices were also guided by the quality and amount of reading material available on the topic and the extent to which the topics provided opportunities for developing the skills targeted in the components. Some themes were designed to span a week and others were extended over several weeks to allow in-depth exploration. Examples included Ancient Egypt, Football, Australia, Space, World War II, Seaside, Films and Archaeology.

PASSAGE CHOICE

To identify possible passages we searched local libraries, children's bookshops and Internet sites for suitable material. In addition, we asked for recommendations from teachers and educational professionals. Many factors influenced the selection of passages and these are summarised below.

For all programmes:

- Passages were chosen to be engaging and motivating; humorous passages were often chosen to promote enjoyment.
- Passages were typically short because the reading and listening time was usually only a few minutes.
- When longer passages were used, care was taken to choose those that could be adapted easily and split into shorter extracts or episodes.
- Passages were chosen to be relevant to children's lives and interests so that links could be made with prior knowledge and personal experience.

For the Oral Language programme:

- Passages would ideally include or be able to clearly link to tier two target words (see Chapter 5 for further details).

- Passages would ideally include or be able to link to examples of figurative language.

For the Text Level programme:

- Complex passages, in which information was not explicitly stated, were chosen to provide clear examples of different types of inference.
- Passages with multiple characters were selected to support evaluative inferencing and the use of theory of mind skills.
- Passages with rich descriptions were chosen to support picture making.

For the Combined programme, all of the above criteria were considered in choosing appropriate passages.

The majority of passages were from published books because we wanted them to be comparable with the types of reading material that the children were encountering in school. Where it was not possible to find a text that met these criteria we created our own. We were fortunate to have Angela Harrington, a teacher and skilled writer, as part of our research team and she created a bespoke extended story for the Oral Language programme. Several of the short passages, worksheets and resources used in the intervention programmes were also written by the research team.

SUMMARY

This chapter has provided a brief overview of the key teaching principles that informed the development of the intervention programmes in the York Reading for Meaning Project. These teaching principles are not particularly new or original; they are well-established principles that have been tried and tested in schools and in research. It is hoped that whilst considering the ideas in this chapter you have been able to reflect on your own practice and draw parallels with activities that you already use to support reading comprehension skills. The teaching principles outlined here fed into the design of the activities and the scripting of the manual as well as forming the backdrop to our training events with the teaching assistants. The manual excerpts that are included in the following chapters offer examples of the instructions that were given to teaching assistants to promote and 'model' the use of the core teaching principles.

With the teaching principles in mind, let us move on to consider the intervention materials in more depth: Chapter 5 offers details and examples of the Oral Language programme; Chapter 6 offers details and examples of the Text Level programme; and, finally, Chapter 7 offers details and examples of the Combined programme, which amalgamates the materials from both of the core programmes.

Chapter 5

Intervention Materials: Oral Language Programme

Typically, children develop spoken language long before they begin to read. As such, oral language provides the foundation for later literacy. In Chapter 2, we discussed evidence suggesting that children who struggle to understand what they read often have wider language difficulties. On this basis, the Oral Language intervention programme was developed to test the idea that if we support language skills, this will have knock-on effects for the development of reading comprehension. The findings of the York Reading for Meaning Project support this idea and you can read more about the findings in Chapter 3. The purpose of the current chapter is to share the fine detail of the oral language intervention components and offer examples of how these can be taught through a range of engaging activities. In our project, we used the approaches with children aged 8–10 years. Nevertheless, you may well find that the approaches can be tailored to meet the needs of children outside this age range.

First and foremost, it is important to recognise that the heart of the Oral Language approach lies in rich interaction and high quality contextualised discussion. Many activities in the programme were designed to develop the child's expression and understanding of language by integrating opportunities for relating the material to personal experiences. In this way, the content of the teaching was rooted in the child's understanding of the world and from there teacher and pupil were able to jointly explore, extend and enrich familiar and novel concepts through

Developing Reading Comprehension, First Edition. Paula J. Clarke, Emma Truelove, Charles Hulme and Margaret J. Snowling.
© 2014 John Wiley & Sons, Ltd. Published 2014 by John Wiley & Sons, Ltd.

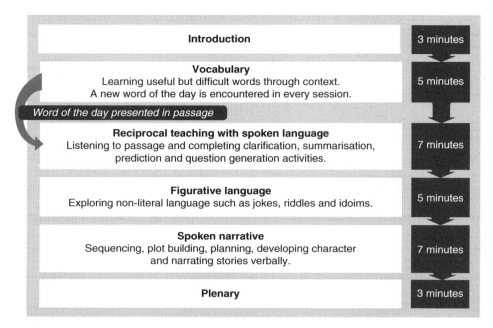

Figure 5.1   The four components in the Oral Language programme

collaborative conversations. Located within this ethos are the four oral language components, which are presented in Figure 5.1.

In our project, these components were always taught within every intervention session. This is because we know that a 'little and often' approach to teaching is more effective than instruction in extended blocks (see the section on Distributed Practice in Chapter 4). By teaching short routine components around a story, poem or non-fiction passage, we were able to provide a structure in which children could consolidate their learning and embed new concepts.

Each of the overarching oral language components contained a number of approaches and subcomponents, which children explored through varied games, activities, worksheets and discussions. These activities were carefully planned and goal-oriented; however, taken individually, their content is unlikely to be surprising or novel to the experienced practitioner. What is novel, however, and what we have shown to be effective within this project, is the *package* of activities devised.

The oral language multicomponential package centres on the teaching of all four oral language components within the framework of the teaching principles discussed in Chapter 4. Figure 5.2 shows the structure for the gradual introduction of activities within each of the four components across the 20 weeks.

As you explore our intervention materials more closely, you will discover some overlap in the second and fourth components of the Oral

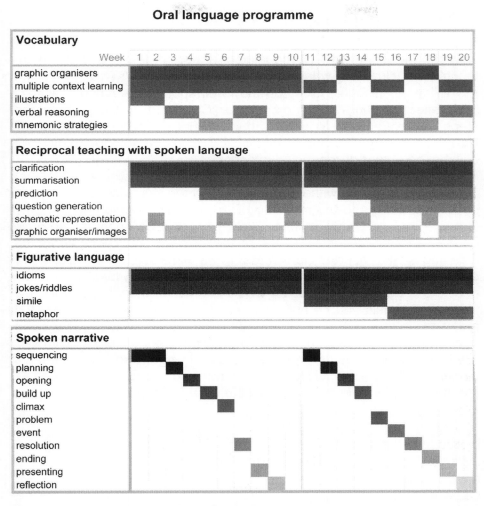

Figure 5.2 The introduction of activities within the four components of the Oral Language programme

Language and Text Level programmes. Both programmes implemented parallel instruction of reciprocal teaching components and narrative; however, the distinction between the two programmes lay in the method of teaching. Oral language components were taught with an emphasis on the spoken word, whereas text-level components engaged more purposefully with the written word.

This chapter will consider each oral language component in depth, with running commentary from Fiona and Tanya, experienced Teaching Assistants who delivered the programme in practice. Their thoughts provide an invaluable guide to the practicalities of teaching and the way in which activities can be tailored for the particular children involved.

1. VOCABULARY

How can we understand the meaning of a piece of text or a spoken sentence without knowing what the individual words mean? Read the recipe for 'Tillimyrie' in Figure 5.3. You may well spot some unusual 'words'. Now reflect on your reading experience. Can you fully comprehend the steps you are required to take? Can you visualise what the dish will look like? Can you imagine how it will taste? Will you be able to produce the dish as the author of the recipe intended?

As you have just experienced, it is impossible to derive the full meaning of a piece of text without understanding the words contained within it. Without access to the meaning of those words, comprehending the text becomes very difficult. Most likely, you will have been able to draw on the surrounding context of the recipe to make predictions about the meaning of the inserted non-words. If we were to give you dictionary definitions of each of those odd words it would certainly help you to decipher the recipe but how robust would your understanding of the new words be? Would you be able to remember them and their associated meanings in three months time? What if we had an in-depth discussion about how the *habirine* was linked to our own experiences? I might say, 'My favourite hobby is fishing. The last time I went fishing I caught a big *habirine* and it looked just like a trout. It had a long body and spots on its tummy. Have you ever been fishing before? Tell me what you know about

---

Recipe for Tillimyrie

Ingredients

4 large habirines, pew into foms
3 tbsps of olive oil
1 hyd of coconut trum
1 cortadil onion, sliced koply
A pinch of salt

Method

Add the foms of habirine to a pan with the olive oil. Wavilem lightly and leave to cool for one hour. If you are in a gnirod a sup will suffice. Gently heat the trum and stir in the minnered cortadil. Season as desired. Wavilem for a further 10-12 minutes until the trum has thickened. Serve on a pock of rice.

Enjoy your Tillimyrie!

Figure 5.3   An example recipe containing 'unusual' words

fishing.' We could then engage in a discussion about our experiences of *habirines* or similar creatures, thereby elaborating our understanding of the word in context.

The importance of individual words and their meanings is highlighted in the first level of the Construction-Integration model developed by Kintsch and Rawson (2005) that was described in Chapter 1. The Construction–Integration model of text comprehension refers to the processing of individual words and their meanings as the first 'linguistic' level and thereby underlines the foundational role of vocabulary in comprehension. Over the years, a large body of research has investigated how we can teach new words in an effective and robust manner. The findings strongly indicate that teaching words in context is much more successful than simply teaching word definitions. Building on previous research studies, our intervention materials were designed to teach vocabulary using the 'Multiple Context Learning' approach developed by Beck, McKeown, Kucan and their colleagues in the United States. Their informative book, *Bringing Words to Life* (Beck, McKeown and Kucan, 2002, 2008), highlights the importance of vocabulary in the life outcomes of children and the links between vocabulary and reading comprehension. The findings of our project echo the latter point in that we discovered that teaching vocabulary also supported children's reading comprehension development (see the findings section in Chapter 3). Thinking back to the example of the recipe, this is not surprising but acknowledging the importance of vocabulary has significant educational implications. Beck and colleagues suggest that the assumption that children will simply pick up the meanings of words independently through reading is misguided. In fact, they suggest that we must explicitly teach particular types of words using a structure that draws on context and emphasises discussion.

What Kinds of Words Should We Teach?

Beck and colleagues propose that our vocabularies are made up of three tiers (see Figure 5.4). Tier 1 is made up of the many basic words that we encounter frequently in everyday life. For most children, these words are acquired easily and incidentally, for example 'house', 'playing' and 'boy'. At the other end of the pyramid are the much less common words, which have limited use and usually can only be used in relation to a particular narrow subject, for example 'allele', 'sodium' and 'terabyte'. Within the curriculum, these sorts of Tier 3 words are likely to be taught in relation to specific subjects such as science or maths. Tier 2 words, however, are rarely taught

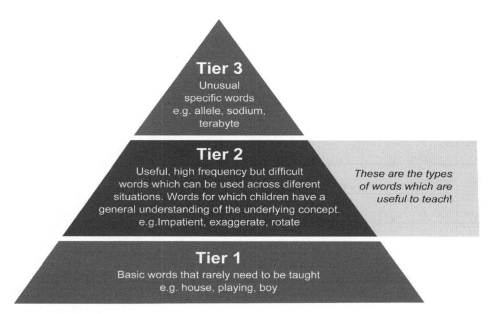

Figure 5.4   Model of vocabulary knowledge

explicitly in school and yet Beck and colleagues emphasise the importance of direct teaching of these words.

Tier 2 words are those that:

* are quite **tricky**,
* are very **useful**,
* can be used in many **different situations**,
* are **important**,
* can be taught in a **variety** of ways,
* are based on **encountered concepts** about which the child has a general, but not specific, understanding.

Some examples of Tier 2 words include:

* *Impatient*
* *Exaggerate*
* *Rotate*
* *Typical*
* *Persistent*

Figure 5.4 provides some examples of words in the three tiers, but these are illustrative and it is important to note that words within the tiers are

Figure 5.5 Teaching Tier 2 words activates and enriches the child's understanding of a number of other words that are linked to their understanding of the target word. This can be characterised as a cascading effect akin to a fountain

not fixed. For a given child, a particular set of words may be considered to fit within these tiers and these may differ from those of his or her classmates and may alter over time.

Therefore, choosing the right words to teach requires an understanding of the types of words that should be targeted. By targeting tricky Tier 2 words, we can elaborate and enrich the depth of the child's understanding of a large number of related words. This process might be characterised as a fountain, in which the Tier 2 word seated at the source has a cascading effect on the activation of a number of words that have a semantic link for that child (see Figure 5.5).

After Choosing the Word, How Is It Taught?

In our intervention sessions, we taught a 'word of the day' in every session. The basic approach to teaching always followed the same procedure and was based upon the *Multiple Context Learning* approach. In the manual, teaching assistants were provided with a script for teaching

Box 5.1   Manual section

Vocabulary activity

Word of the Day: **advice** (noun)

- **Say** '*Today we are going to learn a new word. The word of the day is advice*'.
- **Write** the word on the board and (circle) it.
- **Say** '*Can you say advice?*' Encourage children to **repeat** the word.
- **Ask** 'Has anyone heard the word *advice* before?' **Discuss** the context of the word and encourage the child to draw on their experiences and ideas.

The following questions may be helpful:

  ○ Have you heard the word before?
  ○ What does the word sound like?
  ○ Have you seen the word before?
  ○ What does the word look like?
  ○ What might the word mean?
  ○ When might we use the word?

- **Give definition. Say** '*to give advice means to tell a person what you think he or she should do usually based on a piece of information or past experience*'.
- **Give your own examples** of advice you have given or received. **Ask the children to talk about their own experiences of the word 'advice'. Say** '*can you think of any advice you have given somebody, or any advice that somebody has given you?*'

the word of the day. Box 5.1 shows an excerpt of the manual script for vocabulary teaching.

Supplementary Activities

A number of additional activities can be introduced around the script for vocabulary teaching in order to consolidate new word learning and maintain children's engagement. In our project we used a number of activities that have an evidence base in the research literature. These included the use of pictures and photographs, mind maps (graphic organisers), memory aids (mnemonics) and verbal reasoning exercises such as thinking of words that mean the same or the opposite (synonyms and antonyms).

Who do you admire?

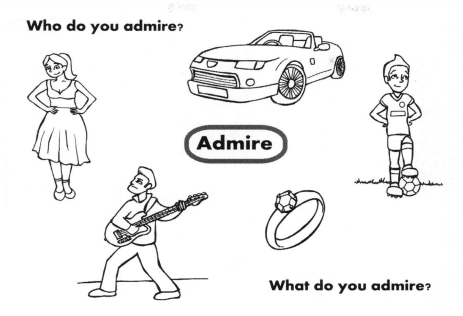

Admire

What do you admire?

Figure 5.6 Picture prompt card for teaching the Tier 2 word 'Admire'

Pictures and Photographs

The use of pictures and photographs to support word learning can be particularly helpful in the early stages of vocabulary instruction. We used collections of pictures to provide concrete contextual cues to support word learning. Hence, discussion was based around the picture prompts and children were not required to draw on their own experiences without support. Picture prompts also relieved the pressure on the teaching assistant when trying to scaffold a discussion around a word that the child had no idea about or to which the child did not have the confidence to apply their reasoning skills.

Figure 5.6 shows a picture prompt card for the word 'admire'. Here you can see that the pictures were drawn from a number of contexts to stimulate a rounded discussion and to increase the likelihood that one of the pictures would be a prompt that would allow the child to reflect on their personal experience with the word.

Mind Maps

Mind maps, also known as graphic organisers, provided an extremely useful and effective means of structuring a child's understanding of a new word. A basic mind map is shown in Figure 5.7.

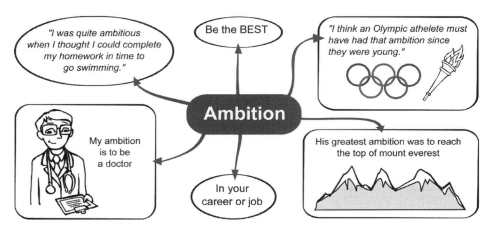

Figure 5.7   An example of a basic mind map for the Tier 2 word 'Ambition'

Box 5.2   TA commentary

Mind mapping worked well on many levels. In the context of Word of the Day, once the initial idea had been demonstrated on the whiteboard, the children were always keen to help add further ideas. In the paired sessions, one child would be writing their idea on the mind map I had started, while the other child was thinking of another idea for when it was their turn. In general, we could have spent a lot longer on this activity as the children really enjoyed it and could always think of more ideas (and later synonyms/antonyms) than the time allowed. Having grasped the idea of the word, some were able to start inserting the word into the narrative activity of the same session. Their understanding was further demonstrated by how many words and meanings they were able to remember in the vocabulary review later in the intervention.

Over time, children could be encouraged to develop mind maps for themselves and to increase the complexity of the structure of their mind maps. Developing children's confidence around mind mapping and their ability to explain their mind maps to other people was an important aspect of the activity. As children's confidence grew, we hoped that they would be able to use the strategy independently to support their understanding of novel words encountered in situations outside the teaching context.

A number of different mind map structures were developed as models and the children were encouraged to use these as inspiration for their own mind maps to support word learning. Mind mapping was also used at the passage level and is discussed later in this chapter in relation to reciprocal teaching (the second component of the Oral Language programme). In the reciprocal teaching section you will find a poster that we used to support mind mapping; this details a variety of mind map structures.

Memory Aids

As a further supplementary activity to aid recall of new words, we used visual memory aids (or visual mnemonics), drawing on children's imaginative skills. Mnemonics can provide excellent clues to the meaning of a word and, with practise, children can begin to develop more complex memory aids. Children required varying amounts of scaffolding of this activity, depending on their imaginative skills and also how aware they were of their own memory strategies. Initially, we encouraged teaching assistants and pupils to work together to develop personalised mnemonics for each word (see Figure 5.8). Over time, children demonstrated great insight into the workings of their own visual memories and usually enjoyed the opportunity to draw.

Figure 5.8 An example of a memory aid to support new word learning

Box 5.3   TA commentary

The children always enjoyed the chance to draw in any activity. The idea of a mnemonic took a little explaining but, with examples being illustrated on cards, they soon got the idea. This worked well with the 8–10 year old children but not so well with the 7 year olds when I adapted the programme for children in year 3 after the research was complete. The 7 year olds found it more difficult to think of ideas to draw and their ability to draw was more limited.

EXAGGERATE	
SYNONYMS	**ANTONYMS**
Embelish	Understate
Over do it	Play it down
Tell a man a 'tall story'	Minimize
Make a mountain out of a molehill	Hide your light under a bushel

Figure 5.9   An example of a verbal reasoning activity around a Tier 2 word

Verbal Reasoning

As children became more adept at learning new words and developing rich representations of those words, we introduced a verbal reasoning activity to extend their comprehension. This activity involved generating a list of words that have a similar meaning (synonyms) and words that have the opposite meaning (antonyms), as shown in Figure 5.9.

We can see in this example how it is easy to make links between this activity and another oral language component, figurative language. For example, the exploration of the meaning of the phrase 'to make a mountain out of a molehill' can take a very similar form to the Multiple Context Learning approach we have so far applied to individual words. Later in this chapter we explore the figurative language component in greater depth.

Summary of Vocabulary

In this section we have considered the usefulness of using a range of strategies to teach tricky, but useful, words (also known as Tier 2 words). We have considered the importance of drawing on context and familiar experiences as an effective method of engaging children in robust vocabulary instruction. We have underscored the value of the Multiple Context Learning approach (Beck, McKeown and Kucan, 2002) to word learning and the ways in which we implemented the approach in our Oral Language intervention programme. We have also discussed a number of activities that were integrated into this approach to provide variety and equip children with a range of strategies to support word learning. Supplementary activities included the use of pictures, mind maps, memory aids and reasoning skills. Taken together, we hoped that equipping children with word learning strategies would support the generalisation of their skills to novel contexts and encourage the adoption of a more proactive approach to understanding new words that are encountered in daily life.

Within the intervention programme, a new word was introduced in every session and it is important to note that the word of the day was then integrated into the passage for the next part of the session. Building in the opportunity for consolidation of word learning within a story, poem or piece of non-fiction was an essential part of our 'package' approach; it was intended that children perceived activities from each of the theoretically separate components to flow from one to the next, with links made across components.

Box 5.4 TA commentary

I soon found that the children were coming to sessions very keen to know what the Word of the Day would be. It wasn't long before they were finding ways of introducing the language into their own stories, and were adding them to their story planning sheets so they would remember to use them.

2. RECIPROCAL TEACHING WITH SPOKEN LANGUAGE

The reciprocal teaching approach developed by Palinscar and Brown (1984) was described in Chapter 4. You may recall that this instructional approach champions a rich dialogue between tutor and pupil in which scaffolding is faded out over time and the pupil is encouraged increasingly to swap roles with the tutor. As such, the reciprocal teaching approach promotes the autonomy of the learner and aims to build the child's skills, self-esteem and confidence around comprehension and oral expression. The reciprocal teaching approach advocates the importance of four key strategies to support the pupil's understanding: clarifying, summarising, predicting and questioning (see Figure 4.1 in Chapter 4).

These strategies were integrated into the second component of all intervention programmes in which the story, poem or piece of non-fiction was introduced. The core difference between the Oral Language programme and the Text Level programme was the domain in which the reading material was presented and the activities carried out. In the Oral Language programme, the passage of the day was presented for children to listen to, rather than read themselves, in line with the emphasis of the programme on oral language.

Listening to spoken passages is quite different from reading passages either aloud or silently. Additional cues are available when listening to pieces of text; these include intonation, facial expression and gesture, all of which may help to support comprehension. There are also a number of other features of spoken language that are not present when reading. Importantly, the process of listening is an 'online' process such that, without interrupting the speaker, there is no opportunity to go back to an earlier part of the passage or to re-listen to a confusing section. Listening to passages therefore makes heavy demands on working memory (the ability to hold information in mind whilst manipulating other information).

In the Oral Language programme, the aural presentation of stories, poems or pieces of non-fiction usually involved the teaching assistant reading aloud the passage or, less often, children listening to a recorded passage. Following this, one or more of the four reciprocal teaching strategies (clarification, summarisation, prediction, question generation) was then introduced using a variety of activities, predominantly presented in the spoken domain. In addition to the four reciprocal teaching strategies, complementary activities were also used to activate the child's background knowledge and to develop the child's ability to build visual representations of passages (using mind maps, schematic representations and images).

In this chapter we explore some of the activities used to support the core listening comprehension section in the Oral Language intervention programme (please refer to Chapter 4 for more details on the theoretical background of these activities).

Clarification

When listening to a piece of text, the ways in which children can clarify their understanding have some similarities and some differences with the processes a child might use when reading the material themselves. For example, just as in reading, the child can use the available context to clarify their comprehension of spoken words or sentences; however, in contrast to reading, the synthesis of information needs to occur 'online' and in the moment. For some children, this presents a significant challenge and the process of clarifying aspects of the passage that are not fully understood might be lost given the speed and transitory nature of the aural passage. Considering our discussion of standards of coherence in Chapter 1, if the threshold for understanding is quite low, a child may fail to recognise that their understanding has broken down in some way or be inclined to allow misunderstandings to be left without further clarification.

In the Oral Language programme, it was necessary to introduce an explicit and somewhat artificial strategy to support the clarification process. Our assumption was that, over time, this explicit concrete aid would be replaced by an internal representation of the need to clarify any vocabulary, sentences or concepts in a passage that are not fully understood. We chose to introduce the process of raising hands when some aspect of the passage was confusing and required clarification. This is just one way in which the teacher can encourage the pupil to acknowledge when comprehension has broken down. In our project, teaching assistants were given flexibility to choose a personal gesture (in conjunction with the children) to make this activity more fun and meaningful. Alternatively, a more concrete aid such as a sign or traffic light system could be effective.

Modelling was an important part of the teaching process for clarification in the spoken domain. It was important that the teaching assistant modelled the use of this strategy to indicate to the child that asking for clarification and admitting you do not understand is not only acceptable but is actively encouraged. This was the core message of the clarification component.

Box 5.5 TA commentary

The children enjoyed being able to have the time to discuss what they had read, and quite often found that they had misunderstood a phrase or sentence and soon started to see that being able to talk about it helped greatly.

Summarisation

The importance of summarisation is discussed in Chapter 4 and it appears to be a critical skill in the comprehension process. The ability to draw out key themes and establish the 'take away message' of a piece of text requires the synthesis of information and the ability to prioritise core ideas over more peripheral information. For some, this global understanding is achieved seemingly 'automatically'; however, for many this is a skill that is difficult to master and therefore requires direct instruction and teaching support.

The reciprocal teaching component of the Oral Language programme paralleled that of the Text Level programme. What distinguished them from one another was the way in which the material was presented and the extent to which children spoke and listened rather than read and wrote. When summarising a piece of text, which has been listened to and for which there is no printed text to work with, the nature of summarisation activities differs substantially from those connected to reading.

Again, the emphasis on oral expression and active listening was key to developing the child's ability to summarise information effectively in listening comprehension. Furthermore, the role of pair work was significant here as there was a need to develop the child's skills, not only in producing a verbal summary but also in critically reflecting on someone else's summary. Together, with the assistance of a skilled teaching assistant, children worked in pairs to build confidence and develop their oral language and critical reflection skills; we anticipated this to have knock-on effects to comprehension because children were not only required to pull out salient ideas but also to communicate these ideas effectively to others. Akin to the emphasis on swapping roles with the teacher over time, the opportunity to summarise information to support the understanding of another person required a deeper level of comprehension than simply drawing out the main points for oneself. The activity was enhanced by the opportunity to receive immediate feedback about positive aspects of the summary and areas for improvement.

Many of the oral language activities in this component centred around developing verbal summarisation skills and building an awareness of the importance of being able to listen to information and tell someone else about it in a concise and appropriate way. Teaching assistants played a central role in this activity and therefore few resources and worksheets were required.

Prediction

Prediction is an important aspect of understanding because it provides an anticipated framework in which the child can embed new information. To predict sensibly what might happen next, the child is required to synthesise what is already known about the passage with their background knowledge

Box 5.6   TA commentary

In the beginning, the summarisation activity was a lightening sketch of the story, which helped the children to verbalise what they had heard so far. This progressed to flow diagrams with missing words that formed a short summary, gradually scaffolding the summarisation process until the child was able to come up with a short summary of his/her own.

It was an amazing transformation to observe: from the difficulties of at first producing a one sentence summary, to hearing a full chapter summarisation from a previous week's text, as part of a continuing story towards the end of the programmes.

about the world. This activation and integration of existing knowledge is consistent with the concept of a situation model, which forms part of the Construction-Integration framework (Kintsch and Rawson, 2005) introduced in Chapter 1. To a large extent, the validity of predictions is of limited importance; in fact, what can be considered to be particularly valuable is the proactive approach to comprehension that this strategy fosters.

Prediction activities were introduced five weeks into the 20-week programme when children had engaged in and practised clarification and summarisation activities a number of times. Unlike the previous two reciprocal teaching strategies, prediction activities in the Oral Language programme were largely similar to those in the Text Level programme except that predictions were verbalised rather than written. A number of prompts and games were used to support the prediction process and add an element of fun. Figure 5.10 provides an example of a simple prediction game that was popular with the children.

Prediction Bingo is an easy game to prepare and can be adapted for use with any text or passage. Ordinarily the bingo tickets on page 2 would include prediction questions about the passage that is encountered in the session. For example:

- What do you think Character A will do next?
- How long to do you think it will take A to get to X?
- Why do you think X?
- How do you think A will be feeling in the next chapter?

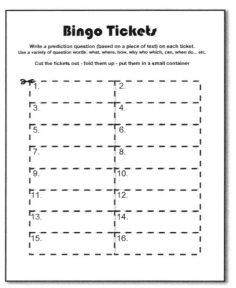

Figure 5.10   Prediction Bingo

- Who do you think might …?
- How do you think the story will end?
- Do you think the ending will have a twist? What might the twist be?

These questions are simply a selection and when using Prediction Bingo in our intervention programmes we were always sure to tailor questions to the passage at hand. Using the bingo tickets, prediction could be approached from a number of angles and children generally enjoyed the 'unpredictability' of the prediction questions! The idea of the game is simple. Children select a bingo ticket and are required to answer the prediction question in order to place a counter on the corresponding number on the board. When a line of four is achieved, the player/s shout 'BINGO!' and win the game. In our project, the game was played in pairs but this prediction activity can easily be adapted for groups. Furthermore, a competitive or collaborative approach can be encouraged.

As children become accustomed to making predictions, they may be able to give feedback on the predictions of others and help the teacher to decide whether the prediction is deserving of a counter. On almost all occasions the prediction made by the child will achieve a counter because prediction questions have no right or wrong answer! This aspect of the prediction exercise can be quite liberating for children and allows for some interesting, fun and quirky answers to be used. As children become more skilled at predicting, the teacher can introduce the concept of probability and encourage reflection upon the likelihood that the prediction might actually be realised.

Box 5.7 TA commentary

The children loved Prediction Bingo! The pace of this part of the lesson really increased with their enthusiasm to finish the game and shout 'Bingo!' They showed a real understanding of the text and their predictions were both plausible and sensible.

Within the intervention programmes, stories and non-fiction passages were followed across the course of one week (three sessions), four weeks or six weeks at different points within the programmes. Therefore, prediction exercises could be revisited in subsequent sessions, allowing opportunities for reflection on whether or not a prediction was fulfilled or discounted. Revisiting predictions can be helpful in supporting the child's memory for the passage over time and provides a further source of motivation to listen to the next part of the passage.

Question Generation

The most sophisticated and challenging of the four reciprocal teaching strategies is generating questions about the passage that has been encountered. Asking a skilled question of a peer or teaching assistant can deepen the child's understanding of the passage because the content has to be considered in depth from more than one angle.

To ask a 'good' question, the child must:

- understand the passage at the global level;
- be able to select an area for questioning that is not obvious to the respondent (and therefore reflect on the level of difficulty for the respondent);
- understand the answer;
- convert the answer into a question;
- ask the question with confidence;
- understand when the person has given a correct answer (even if the wording differs from the passage or from their own use of language);
- understand when the person has given an incorrect answer and give feedback or prompts to support the person to find the correct answer.

Clearly, then, the process of questioning is complex and draws upon a number of skills in comprehension and oral expression. For this reason, we chose to introduce questioning activities halfway through the 20-week intervention when children were familiar and comfortable with clarifying, summarising and predicting. In practice, it would be important to personalise the introduction of strategies in accordance with ongoing assessment to gauge the children's readiness for learning a particular strategy. Furthermore, we found it beneficial to provide a number of prompts to support the questioning process. In our project, we developed a series of activities and games around the key question words:

- What?
- When?
- How?
- Where?
- Who?
- Why?
- Can?
- Which?

Many question games were used in the Oral Language programme; the following manual excerpt accompanied the introduction of a game developed by the research team called Quality Question Street. In the session presented, the activity was linked to a short poem and instructions were detailed on the worksheet shown in Figure 5.11.

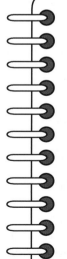

Box 5.8   Manual section

Explain 'Today we are going to play a new game called Quality Question Street! The rules and instructions are given on the resources sheet. Who would like to read out the instructions?'

Check that both children have understood the instructions before starting the game.

Encourage the children to have lots of fun with this game. For example, children could use sound effects and character voices for knocking on and answering the door.

If children are struggling to form questions (because there are few 'facts' in the poem) encourage them to think of questions that tap their partner's opinion about the poem or that require their partner to make a prediction about the poem.

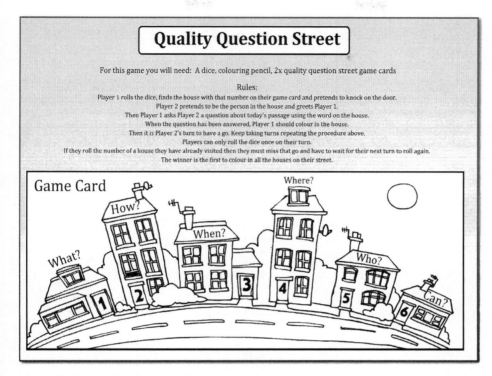

Quality Question Street

For this game you will need: A dice, colouring pencil, 2x quality question street game cards

Rules:
Player 1 rolls the dice, finds the house with that number on their game card and pretends to knock on the door.
Player 2 pretends to be the person in the house and greets Player 1.
Then Player 1 asks Player 2 a question about today's passage using the word on the house.
When the question has been answered, Player 1 should colour in the house.
Then it is Player 2's turn to have a go. Keep taking turns repeating the procedure above.
Players can only roll the dice once on their turn.
If they roll the number of a house they have already visited then they must miss that go and have to wait for their next turn to roll again.
The winner is the first to colour in all the houses on their street.

Game Card

Figure 5.11 Quality Question Street game card

As discussed earlier, the reciprocal teaching approach, which underpins the four strategies, promotes the independence of the learner over time and encourages the pupil to take on the teaching role and vice versa. This process takes some time and, in line with this, the graduated introduction of the four strategies, culminating in the questioning strategy, reflects the transfer of emphasis from teacher to pupil. Supporting children to develop their understanding to the point at which they are able to ask you a challenging and insightful question could be seen as a goal of the reciprocal teaching strand. Some children found this easier than others and needed varying amounts of practice and input to secure these skills.

Box 5.9 TA commentary

They found this very hard at first and the questions being generated were of a simple yes/no variety to begin with. However, the novel games and activities (Dotty Dice Dilemma was a favourite) soon had them generating more in depth questions.

Our experience is that children enjoyed the opportunity, in later weeks of the programme, to challenge their teaching assistant and this activity proved to be motivating and rewarding.

> **Box 5.10**   TA commentary
>
> Each reciprocal teaching component needed to be heavily scaffolded to begin with, but with the emphasis being on repetition, the children soon gained in confidence. This was very evident with the question generation component. From simple questions requiring a yes or no answer, they soon progressed to asking questions of more depth. I tried to take my time over thinking of an answer, even if it was obvious, to instil confidence in the child. There's nothing a child likes better than to ask a question he thinks his teacher can't answer!

Complementary Activities

In addition to the four reciprocal teaching strategies, further strategies were introduced to support the children's listening comprehension skills. These included:

• Activating background knowledge
• Developing visual representations

Activating Background Knowledge

A key strategy for supporting comprehension is to encourage children to draw upon what they already know about a topic to support their under-standing. This strategy is commonly used in classroom teaching practice when introducing a new concept or topic. We believe that this is a useful activity to engage children in, prior to listening to a story, poem or piece of non-fiction or prior to introducing a theme that is followed for a number of weeks. This approach draws upon the Construction-Integration model (Kintsch and Rawson, 2005) introduced in Chapter 1. This model indi-cates the importance of linking background knowledge with incoming information from the text to support a personalised understanding of the passage at different levels.

Let us take an example of a session to demonstrate how activating background knowledge was weaved into a session. In the second week of the programme, a non-fiction topic 'World War II' was the theme for all three sessions of the week. The first pair session incorporated the word of the day, 'Evacuate', with a non-fiction passage about evacuees during World War II. Prior to listening to the passage about the experiences of evacuees, children worked together to create a mind map of what they already knew about World War II to support their understanding when they subsequently went on to listen the passage. We can see how the different activities overlap somewhat. In this case an activity that aimed to activate children's existing knowledge also developed their skills in mind mapping. This illustrates the point that, although sessions were planned in a very structured and explicit way to target specific skills, in reality many components and activities shared overlapping features; this provided opportunities for children to consolidate skills and also ensured that a sense of flow was maintained across single sessions and across blocks of intervention.

Developing Visual Representations

During the project, children engaged in activities that involved looking at images (pictures, photographs or illustrations), drawing mind maps and creating schematic representations. There was a hierarchy to the introduction of these strategies that increased in complexity. Images were useful in early sessions when concrete prompts were used for stimulating discussion and reflection. Mind maps were used in relation to the passage as a whole as well as in relation to specific vocabulary items. As noted in the 'Vocabulary' section, mind maps are incredibly useful tools, which can be developed with increasing levels of sophistication and reduced levels of scaffolding over time. See Figure 5.12 for different mind map structures that can be used to support mind mapping skills. In line with the Reciprocal Teaching approach, the teaching assistants in our project sought to reduce their involvement in mind mapping activities over time and to increase children's independence in this area.

The final complementary activity used in this component was around building schematic representations. Images were used in activities that required the children to think about themes in a more general way and to select relevant and irrelevant images to represent them. Schematic representation activities in the Oral Language programme were parallel to those used in the Text Level programme (further explanation of these can be found in Chapter 6).

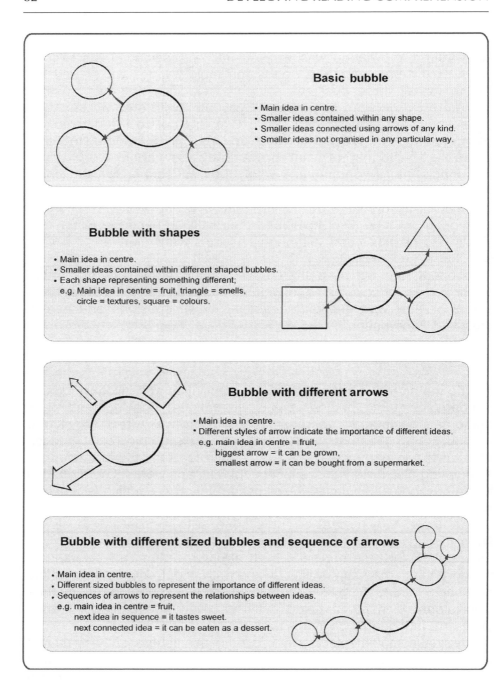

Figure 5.12   Mind map structures poster

Summary of Reciprocal Teaching with Spoken Language

The second component of the Oral Language programme, 'Reciprocal Teaching with Spoken Language', was a particularly central component in which the core passage for the session was introduced and reciprocal teaching principles were embedded in the teaching approach. Comprehension skills were taught through a number of activities, namely 'clarifying', 'summarising', 'predicting' and 'questioning'. Across the intervention programme these skills were introduced over time, with each strategy laying the foundation for the next. Alongside the four reciprocal teaching strategies, complementary activities that aimed to activate the child's background knowledge and their ability to develop visual representations were also introduced.

In the Oral Language programme the major emphasis was on speaking and listening as these skills are known to provide the foundations for reading comprehension. This distinguishes the reciprocal teaching approach used in the Oral Language programme from that apparent in the Text Level programme. In light of the emphasis on contextualised discussion in the Oral Language programme, many activities in this strand could be implemented without the need for extensive resources, worksheets, planning or preparation. The nature of the reciprocal teaching activities, as firmly rooted in the dialogue between the pupil and teacher, allowed the focus to rest upon the teaching assistant's skills and personal reactions within the session. These teaching skills involve the ability to stimulate discussion, model answers, share experiences and offer critical feedback as a means of developing the child's oral expression and extending the child's understanding of passages they have encountered.

3. FIGURATIVE LANGUAGE

Before reading this section it will be useful to ensure you have read the vocabulary section above as many of the same ideas and teaching principles apply here. In the teaching of individual words, we suggest that an approach that draws on context and personal experience is the most effective for supporting children to build meaningful representations. We extended this Multiple Context Learning approach (Beck, McKeown and Kucan, 2002) to the teaching of phrases, particularly phrases with a figurative meaning; that is, phrases in which there is a subtle non-literal meaning such that some insight is required to understand them fully. As adults, we may not realise how often figurative phrasing is used in spoken and written language; however, just take a moment to stop and think

Figure 5.13   'Don't wind her up!'

about the extent to which our use of language is riddled with non-literal meanings by considering the following phrases:

• That was a piece of cake.
• He's on fire today.
• Don't wind her up.
• We had a whale of a time (also see Figure 5.13).

For some children, picking up the intended meaning of figurative language is much easier than for others. Evidence suggests that children with weaknesses in language and reading comprehension struggle to understand figurative aspects of language (Cain, Oakhill and Lemmon, 2005). These children might comprehend the literal, straightforward meaning of the phrase and not pick up the subtleties of meaning. Just imagine taking the literal meaning of the phrases above; suddenly the task of understanding can become quite confusing!

It is important to teach figurative language explicitly in order to support children who find this challenging. In our project, five different subcomponents were covered across the intervention:

1. Idioms
2. Jokes
3. Riddles

4. Simile
5. Metaphor

We will discuss each of these in turn and consider the ways in which they can be taught effectively. It is worth noting here that the Figurative Language component was underpinned by a sense of fun – not just for the children but the teaching assistant as well because this component offers opportunities to explore together the playfulness, subtlety and creativity of language.

Box 5.11   TA commentary

The figurative language components were always a favourite. The children would greet them with enthusiasm as they read the 'Today we are going to…' poster at the beginning of the lesson. We had many laughs over the meaning of idioms and riddles. And when jokes were on the menu, there were usually a few additions that were favourites of the children at the time. Sometimes they asked to copy them down so they could try them on the family at home.

Idioms

Children with the poor comprehender profile often have difficulty understanding idioms and using context to support idiom comprehension (Cain and Towse, 2008). An idiom is a phrase that has an overall meaning that is greater than the sum of its parts. Most commonly, idioms have a non-literal meaning and some are more obvious and more frequently used than others. For example, children may find it easier to comprehend and explain the meaning of having 'butterflies in your stomach' in comparison to less transparent idioms such a 'take it with a pinch of salt'.

Here are a few of the idioms we taught children in our project:

- To turn over a new leaf
- My lips are sealed
- To have a frog in your throat
- Once in a blue moon
- To make a mountain out of a molehill

- To have 40 winks
- To be out of the woods
- Hand over fist.

The core teaching approach centred on learning through context and discussion, an approach that characterizes much of the Oral Language programme. Alongside the routine elements of drawing on experience and engaging in rich discussion, the children also became accustomed to expressing ideas, sharing experiences and making links with background knowledge.

To prompt such discussions, the teaching assistant needs access to a number of useful idioms and where possible needs to contrive or take advantage of naturally occurring encounters of idioms in spoken and written language. In our programme, we tried to include an idiom in the passage of the day so that subsequent exploration of the meaning of the idiom was informed by the previous listening activity. Although this was not always possible, it was desirable and we sought to link the figurative language activities to other activities in each session wherever possible. What's more, teaching assistants became skilled at noticing examples of figurative language and highlighting such examples to the children without prompt from the manual.

We also used published materials to provide a selection of appropriate idioms and a game-based framework for structuring conversations. Two key resources were used:

1. Danielle Legler's (1991) *Don't Take It So Literally!* contains reproducible activities for teaching idioms. This extensive pack of idiom cards offered a scaffolded format for idiom learning in which the learner became increasingly independent over time. The first level required children to select the appropriate definition out of a choice of three. The second level required children to match idioms and definitions. The third and final level asked children to express the meaning of the idiom by offering an open definition.
2. Smart Kids (http://www.smartkids.co.uk/, last accessed August 2012), 'Smart Chute' and 'Idioms Chute Cards', the idiom chute cards, have pictures and idioms on one side and definitions on the reverse side. The cards are available to purchase with a smart chute in which children can post the card into the top to reveal the answer at the bottom.

Importantly, these resources were used within the teaching context of rich personalised discussions.

Box 5.12 TA commentary

Idioms were a very difficult concept for some of my children to understand, and although they knew that the literal interpretation couldn't be correct, they were unsure as to their meanings. It wasn't long, though, before they started to make a sensible guess as to their meanings. The idiom cards were very useful for one particular child, as there was a choice of meanings, and she was able to choose what she felt was the most appropriate. The children were very keen to tell me phrases they had heard Mum or Dad say at home, or had heard on TV the night before.

The manual excerpt in Box 5.13 shows how idioms were introduced to children in the first session of the intervention programme and demonstrates how teaching assistants were encouraged to contextualise the activity. The activity linked to a story of the day, which featured a main character called Molly.

Jokes

The inclusion of jokes and riddles in the Oral Language programme was informed by the work of Yuill (1998, 2009) who has shown that children with poor comprehension skills have difficulties understanding jokes and riddles and that training in the awareness of ambiguity (recognising multiple meanings of words, jokes and riddles) can be successful for developing comprehension skills.

The opportunity to tell jokes as part of a teaching programme is likely to be a winner with most children. Good jokes can be funny or silly and bad jokes can make you groan. Regardless of the quality of the joke, all jokes have an intended meaning and that is often why we feel the need to check 'do you get it?'! Most children (and adults!) would not consider jokes to be part of their school work in literacy; however, the ability to tell a joke demands sophisticated social skills and an ability to understand another person's point of view. What is more, many jokes are centred upon double meanings and figurative language and usually what makes

Box 5.13   Manual section

- **Take out** the <u>smart chute</u> and <u>idiom cards</u>. **Say** 'Now we are going to play a quick game. In the story, I told you that Molly <u>had butterflies</u> in her stomach. Does anyone know what this means? Did she have real butterflies flying around inside her tummy?' **Praise and correct** if wrong answer is given.
- **Say** 'The name for this type of language is an <u>idiom</u>. This means that the phrase doesn't mean exactly what it says, instead it has a different meaning.'
- **Say** 'I have a game that we can play with a <u>smart chute</u> and a special pack of cards. On this card (**select** the "butterflies" card) it says "<u>to have butterflies in your stomach</u>" just like Molly.'
- Pick one child to post the card through the chute and **explain** that the answer will appear 'like magic' at the bottom of the chute. **Discuss** briefly whether they guessed correctly.
- **Say** 'In my pack there are a few more cards like this. We are going to take it in turns to post the card whilst the other person guesses the answer.'
- After each answer is revealed, **discuss** the meaning of the idiom and encourage the children to **give an example** of how the idiom could be used in relation to themselves. Model this procedure by linking the first idiom to an experience that relates to yourself.

Box 5.14   TA commentary

It amazed me that whatever age group tried out the smart chute, they all loved it! Everyone wanted to post a card down the chute even when they had long worked out the simple mechanism that flipped the idiom card over to the answer side. But what was most pleasing was to hear the children incorporating idioms they had learned into their speech or stories.

Figure 5.14   'Where do milkshakes come from?'

them funny is the alternative literal meaning (see Figure 5.14 for an example). Just for fun let us take some examples:

Q.   Why do cows have bells?
A.   Because their horns don't work!

Q.   Why did the crab get arrested?
A.   Because he was always pinching things!

Q.   Where do milkshakes come from?
A.   Nervous cows!

   Structuring discussions about the meaning (and often double meaning) of jokes proved intrinsically motivating for the children in the Oral Language intervention programme because they enjoyed the element of fun. Nevertheless, there was a serious reason for including jokes in our teaching. Jokes provide another example of language in which we must use our background knowledge and understanding of individual words to extract a global meaning from the phrase. The ability to imagine this extracted meaning as a virtual video clip in our minds is often what makes the joke funny. When we explore jokes with children who have weaknesses in comprehension, we find that many jokes 'go over their head' (more figurative phrasing!). Therefore, the Oral Language programme provides opportunities to make the meaning of jokes explicit and to draw out the depth of understanding needed to really appreciate the humour.

Riddles

Riddles share some features in common with jokes but often make greater demands on problem-solving skills. Here, the task of drawing together a series of possible meanings to work out the answer (in other words, to comprehend) is a challenge for most of us. Put on your thinking cap (not literally!) and have a go at the following examples.

(a)
I am tied up at least once a day
And forced to carry ten nails.
I work diligently without any pay
And follow your many trails.

I do not smell very well
But at least I have many eyes.
I have two tongues but I never yell
And I'll bet you know my size!

(b)
I have seas but no water,
beaches with no sand,
towns but no people,
mountains with no land.

What am I?

The answers (available at the end of the chapter) seem obvious once you know them but the process of exploring the language and making sensible guesses is a very useful activity for developing a proactive approach to comprehension. Indeed, this approach has strong links with the prediction strategy we discussed earlier. Thus, although a bonus, finding the answer is not the true goal of the activity. It is possible to engage fruitfully in reflective discussion once the answer is revealed; this has benefits for the child, aiding him or her to understand the intricacies of figurative language.

Simile and Metaphor

Simile and metaphor are perhaps more commonly covered in classroom practice for children aged eight to ten years. These figures of speech compare two phenomena to one another, either explicitly or implicitly; that is, a simile uses 'like' or 'as' to make a clear comparison, for example 'they are like two peas in a pod' or 'it is as solid as rock'. Metaphors, on the other hand, are non-literal figures of speech in which the comparison is more implicit, for example 'the lawyer grilled the witness'. Here, the process of intensive questioning is akin to the heat of 'grilling' but the comparison is not made explicit.

In the Oral Language programme, similes and metaphors were introduced halfway through the 20-week intervention, once children had become familiar with simple idioms and enjoyed the process of exploring jokes and riddles. We considered simile and metaphor to be more advanced subcomponents and we felt that prior experience with the first three types of figurative language would facilitate more in-depth analysis of simile and, particularly, metaphor. In these activities, children were also encouraged to extend discussions beyond familiar experiences to explore why an author or speaker might have chosen to use a simile or metaphor and what impact their use of this language had.

Summary of Figurative Language

The popularity of the figurative language component of the Oral Language programme may contribute significantly to the subsequent benefits it has for children's language learning and comprehension. However, the power of this approach extends beyond the motivation to tell jokes and explore quirky phrases; it is embedded in a research literature that suggests that understanding figurative language can support the development of children's wider oral language and reading comprehension skills. As adults, our familiarity with figurative language can lead us to overlook its importance, particularly from a teaching perspective. However, direct instruction in figurative meaning is important, especially for children who struggle to comprehend and draw out meaning from the surrounding context.

4.   SPOKEN NARRATIVE

The final evidence-based component that was included at the end of every session of the Oral Language programme was Spoken Narrative. This component (and the Written Narrative component discussed in Chapter 6) was partly informed by an influential body of research conducted in the 1980s (Beck and McKeown, 1981; Idol and Croll, 1987). This work investigated the use of visual story maps (representing key story sections and features) to support students' questioning of text, story retells and understanding of story structure. In our study, the narrative component also contained an expressive, generative strand of activity in which children were given the opportunity to consolidate and develop their narrative skills by producing their own stories. Story creation was supported using a combination of bespoke materials made specifically for the project and existing published materials from Corbett and Corbett (*The Story Maker's Chest*® published 2005 by Philip & Tacey Ltd).

As with the second reciprocal teaching component, there were a number of parallels between the activities in all our intervention programmes in relation to supporting narrative skills. What differentiated the Oral Language programme from the Text Level programme was the emphasis on listening and speaking rather than reading and writing. As a result, the focus was placed upon supporting children's skills in telling stories verbally rather than writing them down. As with all the components and activities incorporated into the intervention programmes, there was a theoretical reason for including narrative work in the interventions; this was the suggestion that developing children's skills in sequencing and story structure through telling stories and reflecting on those stories should have knock-on effects for their understanding of stories more generally.

In the classroom, opportunities to narrate stories are generally far less common than opportunities to write stories. In this way, the spoken narrative activities in the Oral Language programme provided an unusual opportunity for children to engage in the art of storytelling using recording devices and most children enjoyed this novel activity. Importantly, activities in the spoken narrative component were much more child-led than other aspects of the session; children were given open opportunities to introduce their creativity, imagination and interests into the stories they told.

The teaching across the intervention was structured around the two 10-week blocks of intervention, in which early work on sequencing laid the foundations for children to create one extended story in each block of teaching. Figure 5.15 shows the detailed structure of the teaching across the 20 weeks of intervention in all programmes.

Sequencing and Story Structure

Across the intervention a consistent visual representation of story structure was provided by the story mountain (see Figure 5.16). The metaphor of the story mountain was used to bring the concept of sequencing stories to life and was extended through two fictional climbers, Billy and Millie, who helped children to navigate the story mountain. Billy and Millie, the climbers, were supported by climbing ropes, which were likened to story threads as a means of encouraging consistency across the story through the consideration of characters, places and times.

The signposts on the story mountain indicated the sequencing of the story. In the first teaching block, children sequenced stories according to four signposts: opening, build-up, main event, ending. In the second teaching block, the sequencing became more sophisticated and children were introduced to six signposts: opening, build-up, problem, event, resolution, ending.

Children spent the early weeks of each teaching block engaging with the sequencing of simple stories. In the first week of the programme, nursery rhymes provided clear and straightforward examples of how stories might be sequenced according to the story mountain signposts; this can be seen in Figure 5.17.

Block 1

Wk 1	**Sequencing** stories (story mountain)
Wk 2	**Story threads** (characters, places and times)
Wk 3	**Planning** of child's first story
Wk 4	**Opening** of child's first story (planned, refined and recorded across 3 sessions)
Wk 5	**Build-up** of child's first story (planned, refined and recorded across 3 sessions)
Wk 6	**Main event** of child's first story (planned, refined and recorded across 3 sessions)
Wk 7	**Resolution** of child's first story (planned, refined and recorded across 3 sessions)
Wk 8	**Presentation** of stories
Wk 9	**Critical reflection** on stories
Wk 10	**Critical reflection** on stories

Block 2

Wk 1	**Sequencing** stories (story mountain) and story threads (characters, places and times)
Wk 2	**Planning** of child's second story (using story planner)
Wk 3	**Opening** of child's second story (planned, refined and recorded across 3 sessions)
Wk 4	**Build-up** of child's second story (planned, refined and recorded across 3 sessions)
Wk 5	**Problem** of child's second story (planned, refined and recorded across 3 sessions)
Wk 6	**Event** of child's second story (planned, refined and recorded across 3 sessions)
Wk 7	**Resolution** of child's second story (planned, refined and recorded across 3 sessions)
Wk 8	**Ending** of child's second story (planned, refined and recorded across 3 sessions)
Wk 9	**Presentation** of stories
Wk 10	**Critical reflection** on stories

Figure 5.15   The structure of the narrative teaching

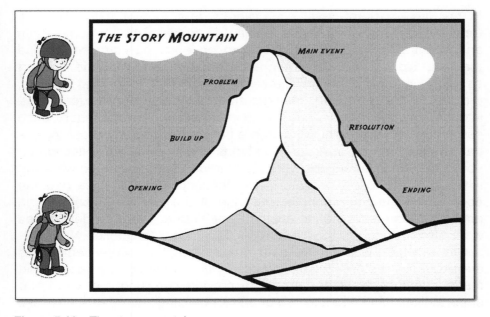

Figure 5.16   The story mountain

Figure 5.17   Sequencing nursery rhymes using the story mountain signposts

Story sequencing remained at the heart of the approach as children then engaged in planning, rehearsing and recording their own stories.

Creating Extended Stories

In the first block of teaching, children developed a four-part story (opening, build-up, main event, ending) in line with the story mountain and spent one week (three sessions) on each part. In the second teaching block, children developed stories in line with the six-part structure introduced in the new story mountain (opening, build-up, problem, event, resolution, ending). Importantly, opportunities for modelling a story sequence were provided in the second component of each session when children encountered a passage to read. In order to support the sequencing of children's stories and extend their reflection on each part, the interventions were structured to ensure that, on weeks in which children were writing one particular section of their story (e.g. the opening), in the corresponding passage of the day, they also read an opening. This meant that, in each 10-week block, two extended stories were also included in the 'Reciprocal Teaching with Spoken Narrative' sections, which were adapted to ensure that they were segmented according to the story mountain in use. This mirroring of the second and fourth components was intended to provide cohesion and to extend opportunities for children to reflect on plot-building.

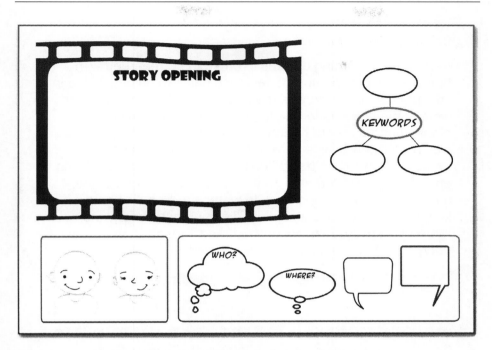

Figure 5.18 The Story Planner used in the Oral Language Programme

Following the development of each story, children were provided with a recording of their story, which combined all the separately recorded segments to reveal the complete story. The recordings provided a stimulus for critical reflection, which took place in pairs and on an individual basis with the teaching assistant. Opportunities to reflect on the first story produced were also fed into planning to improve the second story and children were encouraged to develop their skills in positively critiquing their own and each other's stories in pairs. Questions were used to support the reflection process such as:

• Did the story have all the parts of the story mountain?
• Which part was the best/most exciting?
• What did you think of the story threads (characters, places and time)?
• Did anything happen that you did not expect?
• Was the story clear and easy to follow?
• Was there anything you did not understand?

In the second block of teaching, planning was facilitated by the Story Planner (Figure 5.18), which was developed in response to feedback from teaching assistants informing us that children required a prop for remembering, rehearsing and recording each section of their story.

Box 5.15   TA commentary

Initially, the recording devices seemed to be regarded with fear and suspicion but with each use children gained a little in confidence. One child was really terrified of it and needed to write some prompts for me to point to when her mind went blank after the record button was pressed. But how proud she was of her efforts when she was persuaded to listen to herself afterwards! She couldn't wait to receive her CD at the end of the programme! In contrast, her partner took to the recording process like a duck to water, each section was a lengthy piece full of description, dialogue and usually the Word of the Day! Both children worked very hard and I was really proud of them for what they achieved.

Creating stories over time had its own challenges. Some children found it hard to carry on from the previous week, and even listening to their own recording and using the story planner was not enough to enable them to produce a coherent story with sufficient detail. Others had a very good overall view of where their story was going each session and after a quick listen to the previous week's recording were able to continue with little or no problems.

Had I had the time I would have preferred to build up the story using the planner each week, and discuss each section of the story with the child, then produce a single recording at the end. Another possible method would be to record their thoughts on the week's planning and listen to them at the end before making a story recording in the final week.

Summary of Spoken Narrative

This section has outlined the way in which spoken narrative skills were supported in the Oral Language programme and integrated with other components to develop comprehension skills. The development of children's skills in oral expression was a cornerstone of the Oral Language programme and the spoken narrative component offered opportunities to develop and extend expressive language skills even further. Familiar concrete aids around narrative structure were used to develop children's proficiency in telling stories and reflecting on those stories. In particular, spoken narrative was taught in parallel with activities around a passage to demonstrate and consolidate children's understanding of story sequencing and story cohesion. Children were given opportunities to create their own stories over extended periods of time and this allowed for a great deal of child-led content, which was very motivating for the children.

Box 5.16   TA commentary

Despite the difficulties of writing a story over an extended period, all the children were very keen to record each week's story section and loved using the voice recorder. By allowing them to switch the recorder on and off when they were ready it took the fear out of using the device.

CHAPTER SUMMARY

The Oral Language programme comprises a package of four routine components, which are structured around a passage that children listen to. Children engage in varied activities that focus on vocabulary, reciprocal teaching, figurative language and spoken narrative. The ethos of the programme promotes rich dialogue across all components and children are encouraged to share and reflect on their experiences primarily using spoken language. A proactive approach to comprehending is fostered to support the generalisation of acquired skills to new contexts. Evidence for this generalisation, described in Chapter 3, was shown in children's ability to define new vocabulary.

Answers to Riddles

(a) shoes; (b) map

Chapter 6

Intervention Materials: Text Level Programme

The skills and processes needed for understanding the meaning of text are numerous and complex. In Chapter 1 we described models that can be used to capture these skills and processes and in Chapter 2 we introduced the poor comprehender profile, characterised by intact reading accuracy skills coupled with weak reading comprehension ability. Using this information as a backdrop, we developed a second intervention that specifically and directly targeted the extraction of meaning from text; we called this the Text Level programme. As the data presented in Chapter 3 showed, we found that this programme was effective for supporting reading comprehension skills. This chapter will take you through the different components and activities that were included in the Text Level programme, making reference to key research that informed their inclusion. The programme was designed for children aged 8–10 years and the texts we used were quite advanced, including sophisticated vocabulary and concepts; in our view the activities could easily be adapted for older children. Central to the Text Level programme was a guided, detailed exploration of text. Children were given a 'Reader' containing the passages to read and analyse and many activities were supported with worksheets. The programme comprised four components (see Figure 6.1 below) embedded within the framework of the teaching principles discussed in Chapter 4. Figure 6.2 shows the structure for the gradual introduction of activities within each of the four components across the 20 weeks.

Developing Reading Comprehension, First Edition. Paula J. Clarke, Emma Truelove,
Charles Hulme and Margaret J. Snowling.
© 2014 John Wiley & Sons, Ltd. Published 2014 by John Wiley & Sons, Ltd.

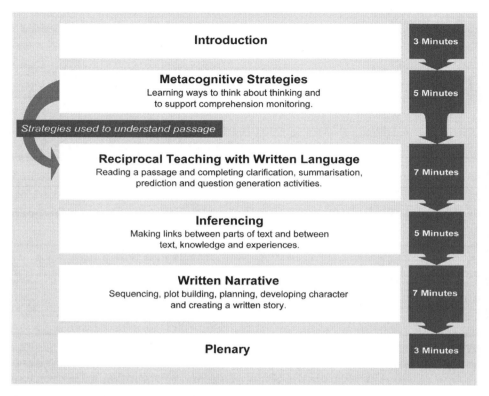

Figure 6.1   The four components in the Text Level programme

This chapter will consider each Text Level component in depth, in the order in which they were delivered. Reference will be made throughout to concrete examples from the programme. As in Chapter 5 there will be running commentary from Fiona and Tanya, experienced Teaching Assistants who delivered the programme in practice.

1.   METACOGNITIVE STRATEGIES

Metacognition is a term used to describe the process of thinking about your own thinking. It is thinking about how you make sense of incoming information. Metacognition could involve thinking about decisions, making links, mental picture making and processes involved in memory. It could also involve evaluating one's personal response to the information and considering its relevance to your own knowledge and experiences. Metacognition also encompasses the ability to monitor the extent to which information has been comprehended and the ability to plan, generate and

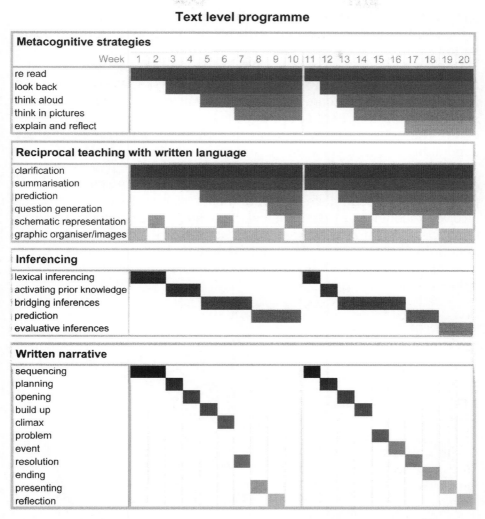

Figure 6.2 The introduction of activities within the four components of the Text Level programme

evaluate responses to others. Broadly speaking, it is the explicit recognition of what your mind is doing and the ability to reflect upon this.

Recognizing that people's thought processes differ, it is likely that some people will benefit more from certain strategies than others. For this reason, we decided that a variety of different strategies would be taught in the Text Level programme. The idea was that we wanted to equip children with a range of approaches to thinking about their thinking. We used the metaphor of a toolkit throughout to promote this idea and to encourage independent use of the strategies. To provide visual support for this toolkit we developed strategy cards for children to keep in their folders and use throughout the programme. See Figure 6.3 below for the set of blank strategy card templates.

Once a particular strategy had been introduced and practised, the children were supported to write a summary of that strategy in their own words on the strategy cards. This summary acted as a cue in later sessions when children were encouraged to use the strategy more independently. The following boxes show the manual entry for the reread strategy used at the end of the first week.

As the programme progressed, the children were supported through discussion and worksheets to compare and contrast the different strategies and think about those that were most suited to them. This process involved recognition of different task demands and developing an ability to decide which strategies were most useful in which circumstances. We hoped that by the end of the programme the children would feel confident about selecting strategies to support their understanding during independent learning.

Figure 6.3 Metacognitive strategy card templates

Box 6.1   Manual section

- **Say** 'So let's recap – this week we have learnt the reread strategy, each time you successfully learn a new strategy you will receive a prompt card. You will be collecting lots of these cards over the next couple of terms. Keep them safe and, whenever you have trouble finding an answer to a question, use the prompt cards to remind you of the different things you can do to help you work it out. We will practise the reread strategy again next week.'
- **Say** 'Here is your first strategy card, reread; let's **write** what reread means on the card.' Help the child to summarise what reread means.
- **Say** 'Every time you use the reread card during one of our sessions you will get a star sticker; let's see how many stars you can collect!'

Box 6.2   TA commentary

The children loved 'collecting' their strategy cards. We used them a lot towards the end of the intervention as the children tried to select which strategy they would use in a particular situation, or to use the strategy which they found was the most use to them. I saved their cards and re-used them in Y6 when they were doing revision for their SATs and needed help with the reading comprehension paper. Once I had reminded the children of the strategies they were soon using them in practice papers.

In total five metacognitive strategies, for which there was evidence that they were effective, were selected. These were taught in the following order:

1. Reread (Garner, Macready and Wagoner, 1984)
2. Look-back (Garner, 1982)
3. Think-aloud (Davey, 1983; Farr and Conner, 2004)
4. Think in pictures (Peters, Levin, McGivern and Pressley, 1985; Oakhill and Patel, 1991)
5. Explain and reflect (McNamara, 2004)

The most straightforward and concrete strategies were taught first and the most complex strategies were included towards the end of the programme. In the first 10 weeks of teaching we covered strategies one to four and in the second 10 weeks of the programme the fifth strategy was added.

Reread

The first strategy introduced in the Text Level programme was the reread strategy. After reading the text, children were asked some literal questions, which could be answered by looking carefully at the text. We noted that initially the children rarely returned to the text and so the reread strategy involved encouraging children to revisit the text and to read it again from the start when answering the questions. The following box provides the manual entry for the introduction to this activity.

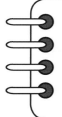

Box 6.3 Manual section

Say 'One way in which we can find out the answer is to read the passage again, thinking carefully about each word. Let's do this; I will ask you to stop reading at different points to see whether or not you have found the answer yet.'

The teaching assistants were instructed to pause after every two sentences and ask the children if they had found the answer. If the children were finding it difficult to locate the answer then the teaching assistants isolated the sentence containing the answer and went through it with them word for word. If still unanswered, the teaching assistant then supplied the correct answer with an accompanying explanation. This process was practised a number of times. When the children used this strategy spontaneously and independently, they were given a sticker as a reward.

Look-Back

The next strategy, introduced in week 3 of the programme, was look-back. As with the reread strategy, work on this strategy took place immediately after reading the text of the day. Questions were posed that again could be answered by looking carefully at the text; however, the answers appeared a long way into the passage. Let us consider the manual entry for the introduction of the look-back strategy provided in Box 6.4.

Box 6.4 Manual section

Say 'So over the last two weeks we have been using the reread strategy to find out the answers to different questions about the passages. Let's use it one more time with this poem. Find the answer to the following question, what appeared on the new white carpet? (muddy footprints). Start at the first line of the poem and keep reading until you think you have found the answer.'

Say 'We have now seen how the reread strategy can help us find information. There are, however, some problems with using the reread strategy. Can anyone think of what they are?'

Possible answers may be:

- It can take a long time to read through the passage again.
- You may miss the important information because you are concentrating on reading the words properly.
- You might forget what you are looking for because you are busy trying to carefully read the words.

Say 'Another strategy we can use which may be quicker than the reread strategy is the look-back strategy.' Give each child a look-back strategy card.

Explain 'The look-back strategy can also be used to help us answer questions and find information. For example, here is another question about the poem, what was the size of a boy's hand? Let's try and find the answer by scanning our eyes over the poem and trying to find a key word. What key work could we look for? (either boy or hand). Once we have found this word we can look at the sentence around it to see if it can help us answer the question.'

Say 'We will practise the look-back strategy all this week and next week.'

Say 'Here is your second strategy card, look-back; let's write what look-back means on the card.' Support the child to summarise what look-back means using their own words,

Say 'Every time you use the look-back card during one of our sessions you will get a star sticker; let's see how many stars you can collect!'

In later sessions, the look-back strategy was embedded into games. One example of this was the look-back race. In this game children worked together to answer questions. The task can be broken down in the following way:

1. Read the question and find a key word.
2. Revisit the passage and locate the key word.
3. Look around the key word for the answer.
4. Find the answer and write it down.

Each race contained three questions to solve. The children were given two attempts at this and each attempt was timed using a stopwatch. The goal was to try and beat the previous time. Emphasis was placed on speed and accuracy and a rule was introduced whereby, if a mistake was made, a time penalty of five seconds was added. In our project, children were encouraged to support one another and work together as a team; however, the game could easily be adapted for use competitively if this was felt to appeal to the personalities of the children involved.

To develop the look-back strategy, children were encouraged to think about synonyms for the key words in the questions and look for those as well. A further extension activity combined error detection with the look-back strategy and required children to read a passage containing mistakes and look back to the original text to find the relevant information needed to correct those mistakes.

Think-aloud

The third strategy, introduced in week 5 of the programme, was the think-aloud strategy. Unlike reread and look-back, the think-aloud strategy was introduced before the reading of the passage. The purpose of this strategy was to encourage children to monitor their understanding of the passage and to develop discussion and sharing of ideas around the contents of the passage. We intended to enrich the children's experience of the passage by giving them an opportunity to provide a personal response to different events, characters and descriptions. The passage used to support this strategy included stars placed at regular intervals. These were visual prompts to remind readers to pause and think aloud. The manual entry for the introduction to this strategy is given in Box 6.5.

To support the children in the use of the strategy, the teaching assistants were encouraged to use some question prompts; these are provided in Box 6.6.

Box 6.5 Manual section

Explain 'Today we're going to think about a new strategy, think-aloud.'

Say 'Firstly I'll show you what it means to think-aloud and then you will have a chance to try it yourselves. I'm going to read a passage and every time I see a star at the end of the sentence I'm going to say aloud what it is I'm thinking. I am then going to make a note of it on the board so I don't forget any of my thoughts. I would like you to listen carefully whilst I'm doing this as we are going to talk about what I was thinking about at the end.'

Read the passage and stop each time you see a star.
Each time you stop, **explain** to the children what you are thinking about.
If your mind goes blank here are some prompts to help you:

Things you could be thinking about (adapted from Davey, 1983)

• Prior knowledge – things you already know about the topic/word
• Visualising – creating an image in your mind of the text
• Making analogies – comparing what you are reading to own experiences or other stories, films, etc.
• Expressing confusion – about a word or sentence
• Backtracking – going back to earlier portions of the text to make sense of what you are currently reading
• Rereading
• Reading ahead
• Using context to work out the meaning of a word
• Identifying important and unimportant information
• Summarising

When you have demonstrated the think-aloud strategy using the three star points, **ask** the children to take it in turns to have a go. **Encourage** the children to listen respectfully to one another.

Say 'Now it's your turn to try. Read your part of the passage aloud and then when you reach the star tell us what it is you are thinking about.'

Give lots of praise and encouragement.

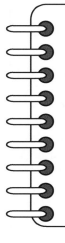

Box 6.6   Manual section

If the child reaches a star and says they're not thinking about anything then try prompting with the following:

- Have you thought about what you already know about the topic?
- Have you got a picture in your mind as you're reading?
- Does the passage remind you of any stories, films, cartoons, etc.?
- Are you uncertain about what a particular word or sentence might mean?

In an attempt to make the strategy more concrete, later sessions introduced coloured objects to represent different types of thought. The idea was to provide visual and tactile clues to support memory for the different types of thinking. For example, when thinking of analogies the children were encouraged to select a red object and when thinking about and using real world knowledge to select a blue object. To encourage independent use of this strategy the later sessions involved reading passages that did not have star prompts, so the children were free to stop and pause wherever they wanted to.

Thinking in Pictures

Thinking in Pictures, or 'Mental Imagery' as it is often referred to, is a component of reading comprehension that has been explored in previous interventions for children who show the poor comprehender profile. A key example is a study by Oakhill and Patel (1991), influenced by the ideas of Peters, Levin, McGivern and Pressley (1985). Peters and colleagues (1985) suggested that to support mental imagery skills children should receive two types of training:

1. Representational: creating pictures that are detailed and accurate representations of information in the text.
2. Transformational: creating pictures that are more flexible and can be edited to support memory for key ideas or specific details in the text.

Oakhill and Patel (1991) devised a programme to evaluate this dual approach, which included cartoon sequences and pictures to capture the events in a text (representational activities) and transformational style

Figure 6.4 The sequence of activities used to support thinking in pictures

drawings (focused on depicting specific parts to be remembered). In the initial sessions, drawings were made; however, by the final session only mental images were created. Oakhill and Patel (1991) found that children who showed the poor comprehender profile benefited more than typically developing readers from this type of support. They also suggested that 'the ability to use imagery strategies may give poor comprehenders a way of helping to circumvent their memory limitations…' (p. 114) and that imagery training '…enables them, or forces them, to integrate information in the text in a way that they would not normally do' (p. 114).

This work inspired us and we used it to inform the activities and methods developed for the Text Level programme. The thinking in pictures strategy was introduced in week 7 of the programme and it emphasised carefully thinking about the information in a passage and working out which aspects could be represented pictorially. The purpose of the strategy was to demonstrate how pictures can help us to understand and remember text. Over the sessions thinking in pictures was supported by (1) looking at pictures and illustrations, (2) completing incomplete pictures and (3) creating pictures with pen and paper. Figure 6.4 illustrates the sequence of these activities.

Looking at Pictures and Illustrations

For this activity three illustrated passages were used. The first of these was used to demonstrate the activity. Highlighting, arrows and circles were used to show how the information in the text and the content of the illustration linked together. The other two passages and illustrations were not annotated and it was the children's task to make the links between what was pictured and what was stated in the text. Each child was given a different example to work from to avoid copying and collaboration. The manual entry for this task is given in Box 6.7.

Box 6.7 Manual section

Explain 'Today we are going to think about all the different types of things that can be included in pictures.' Show the children the demonstration example.

Say 'You can see here a picture and some text about ancient Egyptian life. In the text everything that could possibly be included in a picture about that text has been highlighted. Arrows have been drawn to show where the things in the text are included in the picture. Your job is to do the same with the example on your worksheets.'

Explain 'Before you take a look at the pictures on your worksheets I would like you each to spend a few moments reading the text.'

After they have read the text ask 'As you were reading did you have a picture in your mind of the text? If so what was that picture?' then 'What do you think the picture will look like? What pieces of information might it include?'

Then **reveal the pictures** to the children and **instruct** them to start highlighting and drawing arrows.

After the children have attempted this, ask:

- Is there any information in the text that has not been included in the picture?
- Is there any information in the picture that is not in the text?

Finish the activity by asking 'What did you think of the pictures we have looked at today? Do you think they are good? Could they be made better in any way?'

Completing Incomplete Pictures

In the next phase of the thinking in pictures strategy, the children were presented with pictures that contained only some of the events mentioned in the text. This worksheet provided scaffolding for the activity and a starting point for the children's own drawings. The children were instructed to close their eyes and imagine the scene described in the text and then use their imagined picture to help them to complete the drawing. Recognising that for some children this would place heavy demands on memory, the children were also reassured that if they could not think of many things they could look back at the text to help them generate ideas. After creating pictures in their minds, children were asked to reflect on how useful it was and to describe the quality of their mental pictures (e.g. fuzzy, clear, detailed, colourful).

Creating Pictures with Pen and Paper

Following on from the completing pictures activity, the scaffolding was largely taken away and emphasis was placed on the children generating their own pictures from scratch. Example activities included: children creating a cartoon strip to depict the unfolding events in a poem, playing a game in which the children were required to guess each other's drawings and creating illustrations to depict a series of facts. Teaching assistants provided routine prompting to encourage children to concentrate on imagining their pictures before drawing and to look back at the text where necessary. Children were encouraged to talk about their drawings and present them to the teaching assistant and to one another.

Explain and Reflect

The fifth and final metacognitive strategy was introduced in week 17 of the programme. The teaching assistant first explained to the children what the key concepts 'explain' and 'reflect' meant. The introduction of the *explain and reflect* strategy was supported by a worksheet using the metaphor of a thought train (see Figure 6.5).

Opportunities were also given for the children to produce written explanations. To help reinforce the importance of the skill, explicit links were made to circumstances in which they may need to write down their thinking, for example in school tests and examinations. To support the written version of the activity, a new worksheet was produced based on the metaphor of an ideas factory (see Figure 6.6) for a copy of this worksheet.

Strategy Choice

Towards the middle and end of the programme, children were encouraged to use their toolkit of strategies more independently. Opportunities for revision were embedded into the sessions and the children were routinely asked to name the strategies and describe them in their own words. Activities, games and worksheets were devised to support strategy choice. These resources typically involved answering a series of questions and

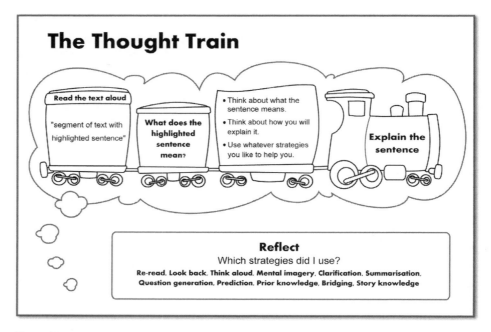

Figure 6.5 The thought train explain and reflect activity

Figure 6.6 The ideas factory explain and reflect activity

then reflecting on the strategies used to find each answer. Children were given a star sticker to put on the appropriate strategy card every time they used one. Attention was also paid to giving the children time to reflect on which strategies they personally found easiest, most difficult, useful and least useful. As a visual aid to summarise the strengths and weaknesses of four of the different strategies (all except explain and reflect) the teaching assistants were provided with the diagram shown in Figure 6.7, which could be referred to in the sessions.

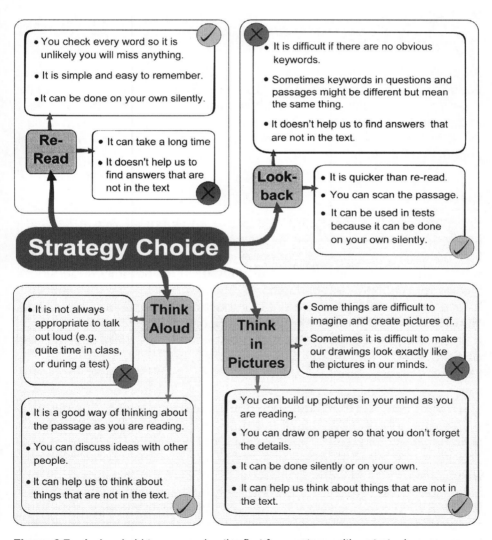

Figure 6.7   A visual aid to summarise the first four metacognitive strategies

Summary of Metacognitive Strategies

To monitor our understanding of what we read and to respond to questions about text often requires us to use strategies. In the Text Level programme the teaching assistants taught children five different strategies and encouraged evaluation of which strategies were most useful in which circumstances. Activities and games provided opportunities for practising the strategies and the children made strategy cards as visual reminders to use whilst reading.

2.   RECIPROCAL TEACHING WITH WRITTEN LANGUAGE

As outlined in Chapters 4 and 5, the reciprocal teaching approach was used in all three intervention programmes. This section provides some details and examples concerning how this approach was applied to text in the context of this study. Throughout, emphasis was placed on ensuring that the strategies were distinct and clearly explained with visual support and appropriate scaffolds.

Clarification

The process of clarifying involves active engagement with a passage and the ability to monitor one's own comprehension of it. The clarification strategy emphasises the importance of listening and looking out for words, phrases or concepts that are unfamiliar or not fully understood. Once identified, the second part of the clarification process involves thinking about ways to make sense of the language and identifying techniques and sources of information to support this.

The clarification strategy was introduced in the very first session and was practised and reinforced throughout the programme. To begin, the focus was on encouraging children to find words that they did not understand. Using highlighter pens, they were asked to reread the passage and mark the words that they found difficult to comprehend. The purpose of this was to support the children's monitoring skills and to help them to build confidence in expressing that they did not understand something. The sessions were designed to be a supportive and secure space in which children could talk openly about aspects of the text they could not fully understand. Where appropriate, the teaching assistants modelled this activity to demonstrate that they also found some words more difficult to understand than others. In circumstances where children did not highlight any words for clarification, we provided a list of 'difficult words' in the manual for teaching assistants to use in order to clarify children's understanding of words that were expected to be tricky for a child of that age. Once difficult words were identified, children were taught how to use dictionaries to look up word meanings. Dictionaries were then made available throughout the programme should children wish to use them for clarification of individual words.

Box 6.8 TA commentary

As part of the clarification section, one to one tuition supported by the poster on how to use a dictionary was both useful and enjoyable to all the children. It was good to see how keen they were to make new language discoveries in this way without the pressure to keep up with a whole class.

The children loved having a chance to use the dictionary, something not often possible within the time constraints of whole class activities. The 'how to use a dictionary' poster was a constant feature in the classroom and the children took it in turns as they worked their way through the process, craning their necks to see what the other had found. Each wanted to be the one who found the treasured definition. Once found, we discussed together how the definition fitted into the sentence/passage. It was a new and valuable skill for most of them.

Summarisation

The summarisation strategy emphasises attention to the gist of a passage and its key ideas. The process of summarising can support memory for passages and help the child to communicate important points to others. For these reasons, the ability to summarise is likely to have benefits for both understanding and expression.

The summarisation strategy was introduced in the first session of the Text Level programme alongside the clarification strategy and was a consistent feature throughout the programme. Children first encountered the strategy as a method for shortening stories so that they could be more easily remembered and told to someone else. Summarisation activities used in the intervention programme were partly informed by the research of Hare and Borchardt (1984), who taught children five rules of summarisation:

1. Collapse lists.
2. Use topic sentences.
3. Get rid of unnecessary detail.
4. Collapse paragraphs.
5. Polish the summary.

The aim of the summarisation strand was to support children to build a mental representation of the text at the global level – the 'macrostructure' as described in Kintsch and Rawson's (2005) Construction–Integration model (see Chapter 1). Many different activities were used to support this during the programme, some of which are described below:

- **Underlining or highlighting key ideas.** Children either worked together or raced against one another to find key ideas. Once they had highlighted them, the teaching assistant read just the key ideas aloud and demonstrated how the meaning of the passage remained intact. Children enjoyed the novelty of using highlighter pens and this increased their motivation to complete the task. The challenge at times was to stem the temptation to underline everything in a paragraph just because it looked nice! However, children soon realised that underlining too many words and sentences made the task of producing a short summary much more difficult.
- **Creating graphic organisers or mind maps.** Very simple mind maps (also known as graphic organisers) were created to highlight and organise the key ideas in the text. Children created mind maps collaboratively and initially these were modelled by the teaching assistant.
- **Shrinking paragraphs into sentences.** Children were asked to read a paragraph and then create a short sentence to capture its meaning.
- **Creating fact sheets.** Children were given longer pieces of text to dissect and were encouraged to identify the key ideas and present them as a fact sheet.
- **Deleting unnecessary words.** This task essentially represented the opposite of underlining or highlighting key ideas. Children were required to focus on words that contribute little to the overall meaning of the text and cross them out. The teaching assistant then read the remaining passage aloud and demonstrated that the meaning remained intact.
- **Thinking of appropriate titles.** Children were given passages that did not have titles and were encouraged to generate some titles that would

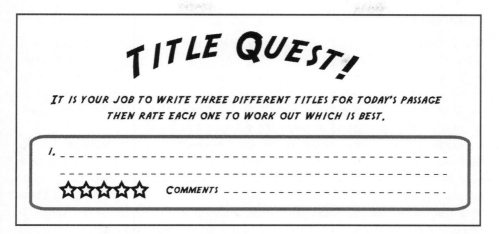

Figure 6.8   The title quest summarisation activity

provide a good summary of the content. They were then encouraged
to reflect on and review the quality of the titles they had created.

- **Completing incomplete summaries.** Children were given pre-written
  summaries that had sections missing. They were required to look back
  to the text and fill in the gaps to create coherent, informative summary
  paragraphs.
- **Selecting important ideas.** Children were presented with a passage
  and a selection of summaries written as facts. They were instructed to
  identify which summaries captured the most important ideas from the
  passage.

All of these activities were supported by worksheets, which were
designed to be engaging, motivating and fun to complete. An example of
a worksheet designed to support children to generate titles is provided in
Figure 6.8.

Box 6.9   TA commentary

Summarising became one of the favourite activities, and
probably one of the skills that was most successfully
transferred into other parts of their school life. I found that
getting children to delete excess information, rather than
the highlight key ideas, often produced a shorter and
more succinct summary.

Prediction

Prediction can be considered as a type of inference-making activity that serves to enrich understanding of a passage. It is an elaboration task that involves the bringing together of different sources of information. In order to make predictions about events, settings or characters in a passage, it is necessary to have a well-developed understanding of the passage, as well as access to relevant existing knowledge.

Prediction strategies were introduced in week 5 of the programme. At first the emphasis was on making predictions about what might happen next in a story. This is a form of elaboration and requires inferencing skills. As such, prediction activities were also included in the 'inferencing from text' component described later in this chapter. These areas of overlap were unavoidable as the complexity of the skills and processes involved in reading comprehension do not lend themselves to neat packaging and delineation. We made the decision to keep the integrity and structure of the reciprocal teaching approach intact and add in extra prediction work in the 'inferencing from text' component to further reinforce these skills.

The initial prediction activities required children to make guesses about what might happen next by using pictures as prompts. Children were encouraged to develop their metacognitive (thinking about thinking) skills by reflecting on how easy or difficult they found the process of making guesses. They were also encouraged to think back to when they had made predictions before and whether or not those predictions came true. Predictions were first made about fiction passages and later about events expressed in non-fiction texts. Teaching assistants were given several examples in the manuals to support these activities so that, if children found it challenging to make predictions, they could model and scaffold the activity as appropriate.

The prediction activities in the later sessions were typically based around sets of probe questions designed to promote the linking of information in the text with wider background knowledge and the development

Box 6.10   TA commentary

The children were gradually able to grasp over time whether a prediction they were making was plausible in view of what they knew from the story so far. It formed a good gauge that they were progressing and gaining a greater level of understanding from the text they were reading.

of ideas beyond what was explicitly stated in the passages. In Kintsch and Rawson's (2005) terms, these activities support building of a 'situation' model of the text (see Chapter 1). In our project, we used games (such as prediction bingo; see Chapter 5) to support prediction skills. We also incorporated a number of worksheets, which typically included images to prompt discussion and opportunities for thinking about the information on which children were basing their predictions.

Question Generation

To generate sensible and challenging questions about a passage, a child must have a detailed and robust representation of the text. The skills involved include identifying a question topic, selecting a question type and question word, and formulating a grammatically coherent question. Furthermore, one needs to have a developed understanding of the difficulty of the question being asked and whether the question is answerable by another person using either existing knowledge or clues in the passage. This is a sophisticated and challenging task, but one that provides a window on an individual's ability to bring together and interpret a passage accurately. Generating questions promotes social use of language and theory of mind as well as supporting comprehension ability.

The questioning strategy was introduced midway through the programme. To support the development of skills in this complex strategy, we provided lots of scaffolding in the form of games. These games broke

Box 6.11   TA commentary

Children found Question Generation to be the hardest of the activites. They enjoyed the games and were able to generate very simple questions quite well. However, all my children wanted to be able to produce a question that the other child wouldn't be able to answer and struggled to produce a more difficult inference question. We took the time to look back at our 'bridging skills' and try to use these to help us generate a more challenging question. Once they started thinking in this way they were able to not only produce a better question but their inferencing skills improved dramatically.

Figure 6.9 The question generator disc

down the different aspects of question generation into chunks and encouraged practise and critical reflection. One of the valuable features of question generation activities is that they provide opportunities for both question creation and question answering; this can be useful for practitioners as a means of assessing children's understanding of what they are reading. Two question generation games that were used in the programme are described below.

The Wheel of Wonder game appeared in the first block of the programme. The game was used in pair sessions and made use of a question generator disc (see Figure 6.9) and a worksheet (see Figure 6.10). The game was split into two rounds and in each round each child created a question.

Children were required to create the questions independently using a question word (generated at random using the disc) as inspiration. After a child had created a question, it was written down and handed to their partner to answer. To ensure that children created questions that were possible to answer, they were also required to write the correct answer down on a separate section of the worksheet. Where possible, time was spent after the game reflecting on how easy or difficult the questions were to create and answer.

The Dotty Dice Dilemma game was used in individual sessions and represents an example of an activity in which the role of the teaching assistant and the child alternated (see Figure 6.11). The manual entry in Box 6.12 explains the rules and how the game was introduced to the children.

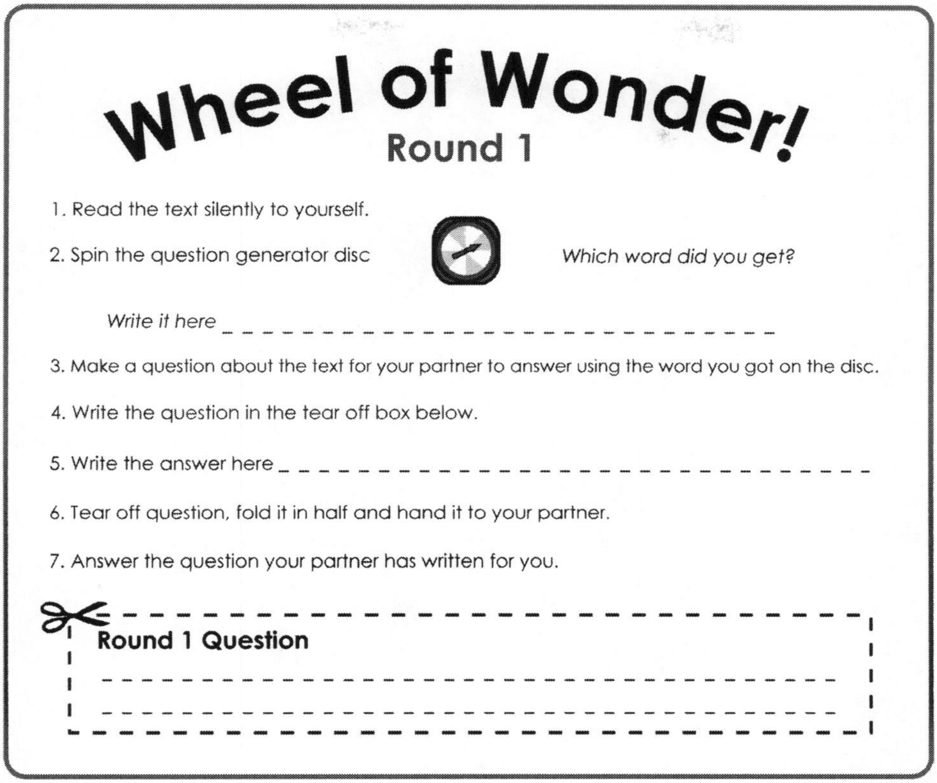

Wheel of Wonder!
Round 1

1. Read the text silently to yourself.

2. Spin the question generator disc   *Which word did you get?*

   Write it here _

3. Make a question about the text for your partner to answer using the word you got on the disc.

4. Write the question in the tear off box below.

5. Write the answer here _

6. Tear off question, fold it in half and hand it to your partner.

7. Answer the question your partner has written for you.

✂ --

Round 1 Question

Figure 6.10   The Wheel of Wonder worksheet

Box 6.12   *Manual section*

Explain 'We are now going to spend a few minutes playing the "Dotty Dice Dilemma" game. We are each going to take turns to roll the dice and ask a question about today's passage. If you roll a 1 then you need to make up a What? Question, if you roll a 2 then you need to make up a When? Question and so on. ... If you roll a 6 then you get a bonus roll! I will try to answer the questions that you make up and you can have a go at answering the questions that I make up.'

Play the game for long enough so the child gets at least two goes at making up a question.

Figure 6.11   The Dotty Dice Dilemma worksheet

Complementary Activities

To enhance the reciprocal teaching strategies in the second component of the Text Level programme, this strand also included schematic representations, graphic organisers and images. One example of an activity that used a schematic representation comes from week 4 of the programme in which children were reading a story that involved time travel between the present day and ancient Egyptian times. To support understanding of 'then and now', children used a worksheet called 'Step back in time' (see Figure 6.12). Children were encouraged to draw a picture of present day Egypt and ancient Egypt and refer back to the day's passage for ideas. This activity required both summarisation and prediction skills; however, it also complemented the work on metacognitive skills as children needed to practice their look-back and mental imagery skills to complete the task.

An example of an activity that used images and graphic organisers is provided below. This was a revision activity that primarily involved summarisation skills; however, instead of focusing on summarising parts

Figure 6.12   The step back in time worksheet

of the text, the emphasis was on the bigger picture and using images to convey what had been learned about the topic of ancient Egypt as a whole. The activity had two parts and was completed in pairs. First, children were required to select from a set of pictures those that were relevant to the topic. These pictures had been carefully chosen to include highly relevant, somewhat relevant and completely irrelevant examples. The second part of the task involved using the chosen pictures to create a diagram. The children were reminded of the work that they had been doing on creating graphic organisers to summarise passages and were encouraged to transfer these skills to summarising the topic. Children were instructed to pay particular attention to layout, considering how images linked together and which of the images represented the most important ideas.

Summary of Reciprocal Teaching for Text Comprehension

Reciprocal teaching is an approach that involves a dialogue between tutor and pupil and in which scaffolding is faded out over time. We have outlined how the four key strategies to support the pupil's understanding (clarifying, summarising, predicting and questioning) were applied in the context of teachers and pupils working together to improve children's understanding of texts. The approach used was a progressive one, encouraging the child to take increasing responsibility for their own learning as they progressed through the programme.

3. INFERENCING

Supporting children's ability to make inferences has been addressed in some previous research with children who show the poor comprehender profile. Yuill and Oakhill (1988) developed inference awareness training that required children to focus on particular key words in the text and use clues in the surrounding sentences to work out and explain the meanings of those key words. To extend this work, children were also taught how to create questions and make predictions about the text. Essentially this approach encapsulated three out of the four reciprocal teaching strategies (clarification, question generation and prediction). Using this approach, Yuill and Oakhill (1988) showed that children could make significant progress in reading comprehension after receiving just six 45-minute sessions of extra support. Following inference awareness training, an average improvement of 17 months on a standardised measure of reading comprehension was reported for children who showed the poor comprehender profile.

Yuill and Joscelyne (1988) developed a different method for supporting inference skills. Children were given a short story that was written in such a way that, in order to make sense of it, many inferences needed to be made. Following this, children were asked questions about the story and given some instructions on how to look for clues. As they found the clues, support was provided to explain how the clues could be used to help answer the questions. After this training, the children were given a new story and questions and were required to complete the clue-finding task independently. Eight test passages and questions were then used to examine the extent to which children had learnt and could apply the clue-finding strategy. A significant improvement in the ability to answer questions was reported in children who showed the poor comprehender profile, suggesting that inferencing skills could be effectively taught using this method.

These studies inspired some of the inferencing activities in the Text Level programme, which was designed to cover a range of different inference types. Brief descriptions of these with some examples are shown in Figure 6.13. The examples relate to the following passage, which was introduced in Chapter 1. For a more detailed review of inferencing training and definitions of inference types see Kispal (2008).

Inference	Description	Example
Cohesive	Based on the text. Necessary to be able to understand the text. Includes anaphoric references.	Who recognised the wallpaper and curtains? – Jennie
Bridging	Based on knowledge. Linking together two parts of the text. Necessary to be able to understand the text.	Why did Jennie hit the button? – To switch off the alarm
Prediction	Based on knowledge. Not necessary to understand the text but may enrich understanding of it.	Which holidays do you think Jennie might be home for? – Christmas
Evaluative	Based on knowledge. Related to the emotional outcome of an event. Necessary to understand the text.	How is Jenny feeling after she hears the news? – Worried about feeling cold and needing more clothing

Figure 6.13 Summary of inference types

Jennie sprang bolt upright. Moments of disorientation followed before she recognised the now faded floral wallpaper and tatty matching curtains. Framed family faces stared down from the bookshelf. 'Home for the holidays' she remembered. Blinking and yawning, she stumbled around for her slippers and gown. The tinny voice from the bedside table was delivering the news and warning of harsh winds and icy roads. Jennie reached across and hit the button. 'Today is definitely a two sweater day,' Jennie thought as she rifled around in her suitcase for her favourite winter clothing.

The different approaches used to support these inference making skills will now be described in turn with reference to examples and activities. In addition to targeting specific inference types, time was dedicated to activities designed to promote the activation of children's prior knowledge and experience.

Cohesive Inferences

Cohesive inferences were introduced using activities to demonstrate missing information in text. Pronoun resolution was used as a starting point for this type of inference making as in general these could be solved relatively easily and quickly, promoting attention, motivation and interest. Other more complex types of cohesive inferences (anaphoric references) were also practised. Anaphoric reference is a broad term used to describe instances when it is necessary to find and use previous information in a text to work out the precise meaning of a word. There are many types of anaphoric reference and the children were exposed to many examples in the passages and activities. In one activity, a quiz sheet was used to scaffold children's inference making. Children were asked a series of questions which required anaphoric references to be made. They needed to look back through the text to find the useful information to understand who or what these were referring to. To support this, filling the gaps (cloze procedure) was used in which spaces (e.g. _ _ _ _ _ _) representing the number of letters in the answer were used as prompts.

Bridging Inferences

We anticipated that the children may find bridging inferences quite challenging and as such the instructions given to support this type of inference making were highly detailed, explicit and structured. Careful modelling using clear examples was a key feature of these activities. Furthermore, worksheets (such as Figure 6.14) were used to isolate key parts of the text to work on and visuals were used as a cue to reinforce the importance of building bridges and making links to form a chain. The following manual entry takes you through the procedure we used, during a pair session, to introduce and support bridging inferences.

In addition to using worksheets, some sessions were based more around discussion led by the teaching assistant. In these sessions, the sentences, children's prior knowledge and guesses at link-making were written on a shared white board. Emphasis was on investigation and the children were encouraged to become inferencing detectives.

In bridging activities that appeared later in the programme, such as 'spot the bridge', children read longer pieces of text and were encouraged to find links between sentences that were not adjacent to one another. The 'spot the bridge' activity was a more challenging extension of the earlier activities, which focused on pairs of adjacent sentences. The skills required to complete the 'spot the bridge' activity overlapped with those being taught in the metacognitive strategies and reciprocal teaching components of the programme. Children were encouraged to use their developing comprehension monitoring skills to identify a sentence that did not make sense because some information was missing. Then, building on their clarification skills, the children were required to scan the rest of the text for clues to help them infer the meaning of the sentence. The children worked collaboratively on this activity, but if they were unable to 'spot the bridge' the teaching assistant used prompt questions to support their investigation.

Box 6.13   Manual section

Say 'Over the last two weeks we have been working on using what we already know about topics to help us understand different pieces of text. Over the next few weeks we are going to use our ideas to understand sentences. We are going to work on something called bridging which is all about linking sentences using our thoughts and ideas.'

Explain 'Now I would like you to listen really carefully as I give you some examples of bridging. Then I would like you both to have a try. Turn to the bridging sheet (resource XXX) and take a look at the sentences and questions. I am going to work through the first two slowly, one at a time.'

Read out the first example 'Sarah took a tablet. Within a few minutes her headache went away. Why did Sarah's headache go away?'

Then say 'To answer the question the first thing I need to do is think about what I already know about headaches. For example, I know that headaches can hurt a lot, that sometimes they won't go away by themselves and that there is medicine that you can take to help make headaches feel less painful.'

Explain 'Now I need to look at the information in the sentences to see if there are any clues as to why Sarah's headache went away. In the first sentence it says that Sarah took a tablet. Now I know that tablets can contain medicine that helps headaches go away. So I can now guess that Sarah's headache went away because of the tablet.'

Explain 'This guess is a bridge that connects the information in the first sentence to the information in the second sentence.'

Say 'Let's try the next one. The cat leapt up on the kitchen table. William put the cat outside in the yard. Why did William put the cat outside?'

Then say 'To answer the question the first thing I need to do is think about what I know about cats and why they may have to go outside. For example, I know that cats can be naughty and make a mess by scratching or pulling things apart; I know that sometimes cats have muddy footprints and drop fur everywhere; and I know that sometimes cats like to eat food off other people's plates.'

Explain 'Now I need to look at the information in the sentences to see if there are any clues as to why William put the cat outside. In the first sentence it says that the cat leapt up onto the kitchen table. Now because I know that cats can sometimes be naughty by making a mess or eating food that isn't theirs I can now guess that William put the cat outside because it was being naughty.'

Explain 'So again my guess is a bridge that connects the information in the first sentence to the information in the second sentence.'

Say 'Now it's time for you two to have a try with the next two examples.'

Firstly ask the children to read out the sentences and question and then prompt them by asking:

- What do you already know about....?
- What guesses can you make?
- Does your guess make a bridge between the first and second sentence?

Give lots of praise and encouragement throughout.

Bridging

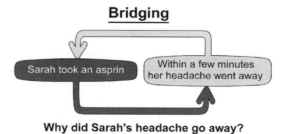

Why did Sarah's headache go away?

Figure 6.14 An example worksheet used to support bridging inferences

Predictive Inferences

As previously noted, the prediction activities that formed part of the inferencing component of the programme were in addition to those included in the reciprocal teaching component. Since we intended for the progression from one to the other to be seamless, the prediction in the inferencing component tended to follow directly from predictions in the reciprocal teaching component; this ensured that the children had many opportunities to practise predicting in a range of activities. We began by explaining to the children that, by making guesses as we read, we can build a detailed understanding of the text. Children were then encouraged to think of prediction as 'making guesses'. An explicit link was also made to the 'thinking in pictures' metacognitive strategy as it was reinforced that guesses can be made about what things look like and that these ideas can help us to build better pictures in our minds.

To prompt prediction generation, a selection of games and props were used. For example, the children made an origami fortune teller from a sheet of paper containing prediction questions about the passage of the day. These questions were used to generate discussion and reflection. In some sessions the teaching assistants gave sample responses to prediction questions and the children were required to use their knowledge to think about which were the most and the least likely. For example:

> James took a sip from his hot chocolate before putting his feet up on the stool to relax. What did James drink from?
> (a) A mug
> (b) A bowl
> (c) A glass
> (d) A saucepan

All of the above predictions are indeed possible but some are much more likely or sensible than others. Following discussion of the various possibilities, children were encouraged to consider 'What makes a good prediction?' and were reminded when making predictions to try to think carefully about all of the relevant available information and use that information to make the most sensible guess.

Later in the programme, attention was drawn to the plausibility of different stories and children were encouraged to reflect on the fact that some stories are set in highly imaginative fantasy worlds. This has an impact on prediction generation as it might be that knowledge and experience from the real world is not useful for making predictions about objects, events and characters that are not based in reality. It is this unpredictability, however, that may ultimately stimulate our interest in and enjoyment of texts. Indeed, in these circumstances, our imaginations can open up to create all sorts of fascinating possibilities and predictions. To support this type of prediction, the children completed worksheets that included prompts to spark imaginative ideas. For example:

What if trees could talk?
What if cats wore clothes?
What if people could talk to fish?

These creative thinking activities were useful in developing ideas for the children's own story writing, which was at the core of the written narrative component of the programme and will be described later in this chapter.

A further type of activity was used, which was based on the work of Yuill and Oakhill (1988). In this activity some of the information in a passage was missing and children were required to look at the surrounding sentences for clues to predict which words and phrases were absent. This activity was presented in worksheet form with a variety of explanations as to why parts of the text were not present. For example, a computer virus had ruined a document, paint had spilled on a page, the dog had chewed up the paper and so on.

Evaluative Inferences

To introduce evaluative inferences, children completed an activity that prompted their consideration of how the main characters of the story were feeling at different times. This activity was supported by a large set of 'emotion icons' – small stamp-like squares of paper each containing a word and small picture to represent an emotion. The activity itself was similar to a 'think-aloud' activity and involved children stopping at predetermined points in the story to discuss and reflect on what was happening.

Another of the evaluative inferencing questions included a prediction element. A set of new scenarios were created and children were asked to use their knowledge of the story characters and their own prior knowledge to predict how the characters might feel if the scenarios were to occur. Children were encouraged to consider how multiple characters would feel in the same scenario and decide whether they would likely feel the same or different to each other.

Activating Prior Knowledge

Children's ability to make links to their own knowledge and experiences was generally supported by careful questioning and discussion. Games were also used to motivate and engage children in this type of reflection and elaboration. One such game was 'Lucky Dip Pick'. In this game, a set of ten cards was used to prompt activation of knowledge. Five of the cards had questions and five had pictures printed on them. Children took turns to pull cards out of the pack. If they chose a question card then they were encouraged to answer the question or give their best guess. If they chose a picture card they were instructed to describe what they could see in detail. In one example of this, the poem of the day was about a mountain and the cards were designed to support understanding of the events in the poem. The content of the cards are described below:

Question cards
1. Can you tell me the name of a mountain?
2. How tall are mountains?
3. What stops climbers from falling off mountains?
4. How fast would you be going if you fell from a mountain?
5. Why might someone want to climb to the top of a mountain?

Picture cards
1. Karabina on a climbing rope
2. Two climbers at the top of mountain with a flag
3. Climbing helmet
4. Cable car
5. Skier on a mountain

Other activities involved using knowledge to imagine and predict events. For example, one of the non-fiction passages included in the programme was about Egyptian Pharaohs. To support relevant knowledge activation, children were encouraged to reflect on what they knew about people in positions of power and royalty. The following manual entry outlines this activity and was used in an individual session.

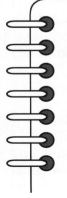

Box 6.14 Manual section

Say 'As today's theme is Pharaohs we are going to think about what we already know about royalty. Sometimes if we think carefully about the topic of a poem, a story or a piece of non-fiction it can help us to understand it.'

Say 'In particular we are going to think about what it would be like to meet royalty. Firstly I would like you to think about how we should greet the Queen. Do you have any ideas? Give lots of praise and encouragement and jot the child's

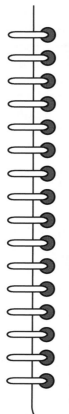

ideas down in the space provided on the worksheet. If the child does not spontaneously generate any ideas provide them with prompts.'

After a minute or so say 'Next I would like you to think about how you would feel if you met the Queen. Do you have any ideas?' Give lots of praise and encouragement and jot the child's ideas down.

After a minute or so say 'Next we are going to read a few sentences about how the Ancient Egyptians greeted their Kings. Let's read it together.'

Say 'Can you think of any similarities between how we greet the Queen today and how the Ancient Egyptians greeted their Kings?' 'Let's think about the next two questions and think some more about the similarities and differences between now and then.'

Ask 'As an Egyptian why would you have to mind your manners with the King?' Encourage the children to look back at the text and consider whether it would be the same today.

Ask 'Why was it insulting to use the name "King"?' Encourage the children to look back at the text and consider whether it would be the same today.

Summary of Developing Inferencing Skills

Understanding what we read often requires us to make inferences – to go beyond the information on the page and draw on a variety of different forms of background knowledge. We have outlined how in the Text Level programme the teaching assistants gave children explicit teaching to develop their ability to make three key forms of inference (cohesive, bridging and predictive inferences) and to activate their prior knowledge when reading texts.

4. WRITTEN NARRATIVE

The narrative component of the programme was more open and child-led than the other components, which tended to involve (at least initially) a high level of modelling and scaffolding from the teaching assistant. We felt that it was important to have an aspect of the session that was creative and flexible and allowed the children to generate and develop their own story ideas. The written narrative component and the spoken narrative component in the Oral Language programme were designed in parallel and therefore shared many features. To avoid overlap, please refer to the narrative section of Chapter 5 for more details.

There are many reasons for including written narrative activities in an intervention designed to improve reading comprehension skills. Written narrative work provides opportunities to consolidate many of the other skills practised in this programme. When writing text, children can experience the perspective of an author and they can then use this insight when they are reading to help them to understand why things have been written in certain ways, using particular writing conventions and styles. Listed below are some of the skills a child may use when writing stories (please note this is just a starting point – you may be able to think of many more examples):

- Produce grammatically correct sentences to ensure that the story flows well and is readable.
- Select vocabulary to convey ideas precisely.
- Practise writing clear and explicit sentences to support the reader's understanding.
- Practise writing more ambiguous sentences that may require complex inferences for the reader to be able to understand them.
- Create imaginative worlds by making interesting new connections and consider how much depth and detail is needed in the text to be able to transport the reader to these worlds.
- Consider characters, places and times and the level of detail needed in descriptions for the reader to be able to create a rich mental picture of the story.
- Consider the emotions of characters and how these can be portrayed in text.
- Develop an understanding of how to create drama, tension and excitement in stories and consequently how to recognise these techniques in others' writing.
- Develop an understanding of different story structures and how these can support reader's comprehension and ability to predict story developments.

It is therefore important that the children can experience being both an author and a reader and, to reflect this, written narrative work was included in every session of the programme.

Summary of Developing Narrative Skills

Children in the Text Level programme spent time learning to write their own stories (just as in the Oral Language programme children spent time learning to tell their own stories). Giving children practice in writing short texts is a valuable way of reinforcing many of the points that have been targeted in relation to reading comprehension in this programme. Arguably, producing written narratives involves many of the same skills as the ability to comprehend narratives that others have written; however, the requirement to produce a written narrative may involve a greater degree of explicit knowledge that is required for adequate reading comprehension of an equivalent passage.

CHAPTER SUMMARY

The Text Level programme comprised a package of four components that centred on a passage that children read. Children engaged in a range of activities targeting metacognitive strategies, reciprocal teaching, inferencing from text and written narrative. Emphasis was placed on children mastering a toolkit of strategies to be used with increasing independence as the programme unfolded so that they could be used proficiently after the end of the intervention.

Chapter 7

Intervention Materials: Combined Programme

In the previous two chapters we have described in detail two teaching programmes that were designed to support the development of children's reading comprehension skills. These programmes comprise different approaches to supporting children's understanding. The first, the Oral Language programme, focused on speaking and listening skills. The second, the Text Level programme, adopted a more traditional approach and emphasised reading and writing skills. Despite the differences between the programmes there were a number of similarities; the teaching principles and overall structure of the programmes were the same and children in both interventions engaged in parallel forms of reciprocal teaching and narrative activities. Figure 7.1 provides a reminder of the teaching components covered in each of the intervention programmes.

By comparing the progress made by children receiving these programmes, we were able to assess which approach would be most effective for improving children's reading comprehension skills. However, we also wanted to assess whether an integrated approach that combined oral language and text-level components would be more effective than either approach in isolation. We started out with the idea that explicitly making links between spoken and written language might be particularly beneficial for the development of reading comprehension skills. By offering children materials in written as well as spoken form we hoped to encourage both more engagement and a deeper understanding of the

Developing Reading Comprehension, First Edition. Paula J. Clarke, Emma Truelove,
Charles Hulme and Margaret J. Snowling.
© 2014 John Wiley & Sons, Ltd. Published 2014 by John Wiley & Sons, Ltd.

Oral language programme
Vocabulary
Reciprocal teaching with spoken language
Figurative language
Spoken narrative

Text level programme
Metacognitive strategies
Reciprocal teaching with written language
Inferencing
Written narrative

Figure 7.1 An overview of the components in the Oral Language and Text Level programmes

linguistic and text-level processes that underpin reading comprehension. In addition, we hypothesized that children's recognition of the common processes used in the two modalities would help reinforce learning in each domain. Thus, we wanted to find out whether this combined approach was more beneficial than targeting listening comprehension (oral language components) and reading comprehension (text-level components) separately.

One of the key considerations for this 'integrated' programme was passage selection. We endeavoured to find texts that offered the opportunity for learning in all components, for example that included tier two vocabulary, figurative language, the need for inference making and so on. In reality many of these features are present in the reading material of eight to ten year olds. Where it was not possible to find texts that already included these features, we adapted the passages.

To support the delivery of this programme we carefully labelled each component with icons, which were used in the manual to indicate when a passage was to be read and when it was to be listened to. We also worked closely with the teaching assistants to ensure that the administration instructions were as clear and as straightforward as possible.

The components of the Combined Programme were broken down into subskills as before. The main difference was the intensity of the work since, in order to fit everything into twenty weeks, children spent less time on each activity.

In the Combined programme, Reciprocal Teaching was conducted in both written and spoken language domains. Every session included Reciprocal Teaching and, by asking children both to read and to listen to passages, this enabled them to practise the same strategies in each domain.

Children also completed both written and spoken narratives. Since the children's stories were constructed over extended periods of time, the first block of 10 weeks focused on recording a spoken story and the second block on producing a written story.

Example: Combined session 1 (week 1, individual session)

Approx. time	2.5 mins	5 mins	5 mins	5 mins	5 mins	5 mins	2.5 mins
Activity	Intro.	Vocabulary	Reciprocal teaching with spoken language	Figurative language	Reciprocal teaching with written language	Spoken narrative	Plenary

Figure 7.2 A Combined programme session: Example 1

To convey the integrated nature of the Combined programme, we will use some example sessions to illustrate how the Oral Language (OL) and Text Level (TL) components were interlinked.

The session shown in Figure 7.2 was near the beginning of the programme and therefore involved the introduction of new ideas and themes. The week was themed around a non-fiction story. The session began with a short introduction, which included completion of the 'Today we are going to…' poster. Following this, the child was introduced to the word of the day, 'Magnificent'. Using the Multiple Context Learning approach (Beck, McKeown and Kucan, 2002) the child and teaching assistant discussed the word and developed a working definition of it. The next activity involved a recap of the listening rules before active listening to the first part of the day's passage. Whilst listening, the child was encouraged to identify the word of the day and the child and teaching assistant took time to discuss the meaning of the word in context.

One of the themes in the passage was 'butterflies'; this was used as a springboard into the next activity, figurative language. The figurative language work was discussion based and centred on the idiom 'butterflies in their stomach', using the smart chute and Level 1 idiom cards as support. To reinforce the literal and non-literal interpretation of the idiom, the child went on to read the next part of the passage, also about butterflies.

Following reading, the child was encouraged to summarise both parts of the passage (the part they had listened to and the part they had read). The summarisation activity involved choosing key ideas from the passage and using these to create short summary sentences. This activity was supported by a written worksheet. The child's summary sentences were then used to lead into the final activity in the session, written narrative. They were asked to identify which parts of the story their summary sentences represented in reference to the Story Mountain (opening, build-up, main event or ending). The session ended with some reflection about the story, which had spanned the three sessions of the week and was now complete. The child was prompted to think about which parts they enjoyed, which characters they liked and whether the story was like any others they had heard or read before.

A short plenary with a recap of the word of the day and some reward time brought the session to a close.

> **Box 7.1**   TA commentary
>
> Although the nature of this programme made it harder for my children to begin to take ownership of the sessions, it was probably the most fun to deliver. The games and activities were very quick to play and the variety of texts were enjoyed even more by this group. The fast pace of the sessions meant we covered a lot of ground quickly. This felt like a rush at first but I soon settled into a routine of selecting which activities we would write on and which ones we could simply discuss so that we were able to complete the session in the allotted time.

The fast-paced nature of the Combined sessions is illustrated in this example and reflected in the teaching assistant's commentary. Every few minutes the children moved on to the next activity but each activity was linked carefully to the next. It can be seen that, once again, the distributed practice little and often approach was fundamental here. Over the course of the programme, children experienced each activity multiple times; however, the different variants of sessions meant that the children who received the Combined programme did not experience the same routine and predictability as the children who received the Oral Language and Text Level programmes.

The session shown in Figure 7.3 was the first in a week that was themed around the topic of 'space'. The reading and listening material throughout the week was poetry. Each session included a poem, chosen to be humorous and short so that it could be understood within a 30-minute session.

Example: Combined session 2 (week 8, pair session 1)

Approx. time	2.5 mins	5 mins	5 mins	5 mins	5 mins	5 mins	2.5 mins
Activity	Intro.	Metacognitive strategies	Reciprocal teaching with written language	Inferencing from text	Reciprocal teaching with spoken language	Spoken narrative	Plenary

Figure 7.3   A Combined programme session: Example 2

The session began with a brief recap of vocabulary learnt during the previous week and an overview of the session to come. The first activity involved learning a new metacognitive strategy: thinking in pictures. The strategy was explained and modelled and the children had the opportunity to practise it with worksheet support. With this new strategy in mind, children then took turns to read part of the poem. They were encouraged to use the reciprocal teaching strategy, clarification, to identify words that they did not understand.

Following this, the teaching assistant read the next part of the poem whilst the children listened. To bring together their thoughts and images of the poem, children then completed a second reciprocal teaching activity, summarisation, using a mind map to record their ideas. Attention then turned from the poem to a short piece of text. In this activity, the children were required to spot sentences that had information missing. They were then encouraged to use their look-back and reread skills to find useful information in the surrounding text to help them to make a bridging inference. This was a quick activity to consolidate learning from previous weeks.

The final activity was based around the children's own spoken narratives. At this point in the programme, children had recorded their stories and were waiting to receive their recordings. In this session they worked on their story covers, using their summarisation skills to think of a good title and their mental imagery skills to create an illustration for the cover.

The session ended with a plenary, which included a detailed recap of their new strategy, 'thinking in pictures', some brief revision of bridging inferences and mind maps and time for rewards.

SUMMARY

The Combined programme included all components from the Oral Language and Text Level programmes. Each session included five components and an opportunity to both listen to and read a passage. The components were carefully balanced across the 20-week programme and the children received half the amount of each of the other two programmes. The order in which components were covered within sessions was varied to ensure, wherever possible, logical transitions between activities and to provide opportunities for linking between the spoken and written language domains.

Chapter 8

Feedback and Evaluation

The York Reading for Meaning project was highly successful, at least as measured by the progress made by the children receiving the interventions. The project provides strong evidence about how best to help children with reading comprehension difficulties – an area where until recently there has been very little rigorous evidence. However, the success of any intervention depends upon its sustainability in the school system when the researchers 'move out'. Whether an intervention will continue following a period of funded research and whether it will 'scale up' across schools depends upon a whole range of factors, including its costs and its ease of implementation as well as how it is viewed by other stakeholders including parents and school governors. This chapter details some of the tools we used to collect ongoing feedback from those involved in the project. Summaries of feedback data are provided; these illustrate key issues to be considered when conducting this type of work and highlight areas for further development.

FEEDBACK FROM TEACHING ASSISTANTS

Feedback was collected at tutorials, through the record forms, and using questionnaires at the end of each 10-week block of teaching. The questionnaires prompted teaching assistants to reflect on the content of the programmes and their feedback gave us a wealth of quantitative and qualitative data. Figure 8.1 is a copy of the Block 1 questionnaire. Block 2 used a similar format but some of the components were broken down

Developing Reading Comprehension, First Edition. Paula J. Clarke, Emma Truelove, Charles Hulme and Margaret J. Snowling.
© 2014 John Wiley & Sons, Ltd. Published 2014 by John Wiley & Sons, Ltd.

BLOCK 1 EVALUATION
What's hot and what's not?

Manual	Rating (1-10) 1=poor, 10=excellent	Positives	Negatives
Themes			
Text Level			
Oral Language			
Combined			
Components			
Vocabulary			
Reciprocal Teaching			
Metacognitive strategies			
Inferencing			
Figurative language			
Narrative			
Passages			
Fiction			
Non-Fiction			
Poetry			

Training, tutorials and observations

Training	
• Was the training given sufficient? • Was there anything we could have spent more/less time on? • Would you like the opportunity to do top up training before block 2?	
Tutorials	
• Did you find the tutorials useful and enjoyable? • Which discussion topic or aspect of the tutorials did you find the most useful? • Is there anything that you would change about the tutorials? • Anything else to add?	
Observations	
• Did you find observations useful? • Were you happy with the level of feedback you received? • Would you be prepared to have an observation videoed in the future (for training purposes)?	
Support	
• Do you feel there has been enough support from the research team? • Have you felt supported by the teachers? • Is there anything else we could be doing to make life easier?	

Figure 8.1   The questionnaire given to the teaching assistants at the end of Block 1

further into their subcomponents (for example, instead of asking about Reciprocal Teaching overall, we sought feedback about each of the four strategies: Clarification, Summarisation, Prediction and Question Generation).

The following section summarises some of the key findings from these feedback questionnaires. When interpreting these it is important to note that the response rate varied considerably from Block 1 (19/20 responses returned) to Block 2 (7/20 responses returned). At the end of the first 10-week block of teaching, the following average ratings (out of 10) were obtained for the themes used in each programme: 8 (Oral Language programme), 8 (Text Level programme) and 6 (Combined). With regard to the components of the interventions, all average ratings were above 6 and the components rated most highly were Figurative Language, Vocabulary, Narrative and Metacognitive Strategies.

At the end of the second 10-week block of teaching, the following average ratings (out of 10) were obtained for the themes used in each programme: 9 (Oral Language), 5 (Text Level) and 7 (Combined). Again all of the components received average ratings greater than 6. The components that received the highest average ratings were Idioms (Figurative Language) and Vocabulary. These were also rated highly at the end of Block 1 and it is notable that these were Oral Language components. The component that received the lowest average rating was Inferencing, from the Text Level programme.

Figure 8.2 contains a representative selection of the feedback that we received relating to support during the project. Figure 8.2 shows that by the end of the intervention all teaching assistants were in agreement that they had found the tutorials enjoyable and useful and that they had received enough support from the research team. The most useful aspects appeared to be training in specific components, supporting one another and the opportunities to discuss ideas and experiences. The few suggestions for change were mainly related to reducing the travelling needed to reach venues for tutorials.

The majority of teaching assistants found having their sessions observed useful. Those who found them beneficial pointed to the quality of feedback and the sense of reassurance as useful features. The small number who did not find the observations useful said that this increased their levels of stress. The teaching assistants mentioned many positive features of the support they received. They also raised many useful points regarding things that could be done to make delivery easier. These mainly related to the time constraints of the sessions and, in particular, lengthy activities and worksheets in the Text Level programme.

Question (% of yes responses)	Block 1	Block 2
Tutorials		
Did you find the tutorials useful and enjoyable? Block 1 (100%) Block 2 (100%)	• Yes, great to discuss with others and to know they had the same problems as me • Yes, very good to meet up and feel part of a larger scheme	• Yes, nice to know you are not alone
Which discussion topic or aspect of the tutorials did you find the most useful?	• Sharing problems/solutions • Knowing that it is okay to miss bits out as long as we get a balance of all the elements of the programme across each week • Exchanging experiences • Talked through lessons before we deliver them • Reciprocal teaching • Ideas to shorten preparation time • Celebrations • Role play	• Sharing ideas • Discussing with other TAs– able to help each other with ideas and a feeling of not being only one having a problem or difficulty • Discussing aspects that were tricky to teach e.g. bridging • Clarifying bridging • How other people do things, ideas to help. Just backing each other up
Is there anything that you would change about the tutorials? Block 1 (11%) Block 2 (14%)	• Only that I wish I didn't have to travel so far! • No – though perhaps an occasional video of a new strategy being introduced (e.g. 'think aloud') would be interesting	• No. Enjoyed the small group. Able to discuss problems, successes etc. • Venue
Anything else to add?	• Never felt that I couldn't discuss anything. Even if I felt I had gone wrong felt at ease to discuss and got great feedback from the group	
Observations		
Did you find observations useful? Block 1 (79%) Block 2 (86%)	• Very useful feedback • Nerve wracking but yes • Yes, if feedback is positive – boosts confidence • No, a lot of pressure, more stress	• A bit daunting at first but useful as well • Not really and very stressful • Yes, you know you were on right lines • Yes, it's nice to know you are delivering a good lesson • Hard at first. I was concerned it would affect child's reactions. Useful to know I was doing it something like it was supposed to be
Were you happy with the level of feedback you received? Block 1 (89%) Block 2 (86%)	• Yes very useful and encouraging • Excellent written feedback • Would have liked written feedback to keep in my development file	• Would have liked written feedback for career file • Would have liked to have been told how I could improve on what I'd done • Yes, although after video taken no feedback was given • Yes everyone was very kind–probably too kind!?

Figure 8.2 A representative selection of the feedback from the teaching assistants relating to support provided by the research team

Question (% of yes responses)	Block 1	Block 2
Support		
Do you feel there has been enough support from the research team? Block 1 (100%) Block 2 (100%)	• Excellent support throughout • The team have been fantastic. Always positive, friendly and willing to help. Always at the end of the phone when you need them.	• Brilliant – always know someone is just a phone call away • Yes, Yes, Yes! Everyone has been very friendly, supportive, lovely, lovely people.
Is there anything else we could be doing to make life easier? Block 1 (42%) Not asked at end of Block 2	• Make the Text Level programme sessions shorter!!! • Yes. More time! More time! More time! For preparation and with children for activities • Allow more space for evaluation of the manual on the next evaluation sheet! • Try to get 2 weeks of manual to us at tutorial so we could do all photocopying together? • Less worksheets and more time for the ones we have? • Yes. Cut down the number of activities per session – make programme less time driven	

Figure 8.2   *(continued)*

THE PERSONAL AND PROFESSIONAL DEVELOPMENT OF TEACHING ASSISTANTS

In the final tutorial, one of the activities involved some quiet space and time for teaching assistants to reflect on their own personal journey through the project. We decided not to use this to collect data but rather as an opportunity for teaching assistants to think about their own achievements in a private way. We gave a number of prompts to support this, as listed in Figure 8.3. Later in the tutorial we gave some time for sharing reflections and achievements informally – there was no requirement for everyone to take part.

OVERALL EVALUATION AND NEXT STEPS

At the end of the project, following the waiting control intervention, we also asked the teaching assistants to complete a final evaluation and 'next steps' questionnaire. This was designed to provide us with summary data, so in most cases closed questions requiring a positive or negative response were used. Some of the questions were repeats of those asked at the end of each block of teaching; others were new and related to future impacts of the project. Figure 8.4 presents the questions and a representative

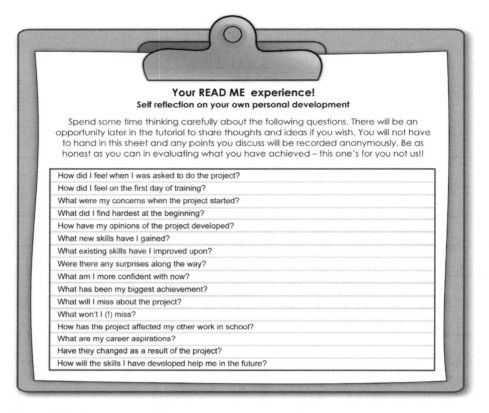

Figure 8.3 Prompts used for teaching assistants' self-reflection activity

selection of the responses from the completed questionnaires (the response rate was 11/20).

The responses in Figure 8.4 suggest that many teaching assistants were keen to remain involved in the future developments of the project; however, some were unsure how much time they would be able to commit and exactly what level of involvement they would like. Most teaching assistants felt that the knowledge and skills they had developed on the project would benefit them in the future and in a number of cases there was evidence of the project already informing the teaching assistants' work with other children and their educational planning more generally.

CHILDREN'S REFLECTIONS

Feedback was also sought from the children who participated in the project using questionnaires. Figure 8.5 provides an overview of the content of the questionnaires given to children following the second block of teaching. These questionnaires were not systematically collected by the

Question (% of yes responses)	Sample Comments
Would you be willing to contribute to future training events for other TAs? If so, in what capacity? (e.g. preparing training materials, leading sessions and tutorials) Yes - 55% Possibly – 27% Don't know – 9%	• Any help you need let me know. I have thoroughly enjoyed being part of this project • Not officially as I have a new role at school, however more than happy to help if I can • Yes, helping with training and preparing materials
Would you be prepared to be filmed carrying out some sample activities for a training DVD? Yes – 18% Possibly -18% Don't know -9%	• No! (sorry)
Would you like to be a consultant in the further development of the intervention programmes? Yes – 27% Possibly – 45% Don't know – 9%	• Possibly – it depends on time constraints and what it would involve • If available
Did you find the tutorials/training enjoyable? Yes – 100%	• Tutorials were a great way to iron out problems and reassure each other • Yes very. It was helpful and good to meet up with others running the same programme • Yes, light and informal but informative
Which discussion topic or aspect of the tutorials did you find most useful?	• Feedback about how lessons went with each other. In the first block of 20 weeks going through future sessions. • Understanding of reciprocal teaching and inferencing • Talking to others about failures, successes and strategies to use in sessions
Is there anything that you would change about the tutorials? Yes – 0% Possibly – 0% Don't know – 0%	• No not really
Was it beneficial to meet up with other TAs on the project? Yes – 100%	• Very much so. Great encouragement
Was it useful to have the members of the research team on hand to answer questions etc. at the tutorials? Yes -100%	• Yes it was nice to be able to ring people up and have problems solved! Also lots of good support
Do you feel there has been enough support from the research team? Yes – 100%	• More than enough – nothing was too much trouble
Have you felt supported by the school/teachers? Yes – 45% Somewhat – 36%	• Yes and No

Figure 8.4 A summary of responses from the teaching assistants' final evaluation

Question (% of yes responses)	Sample Comments
Will the knowledge, skills and experience that you have gained through doing the READ ME project be useful in your future TA roles and responsibilities? If so how? Yes -91% Possibly -9%	• I have already adapted materials to use with a Year 4 group over a 12 week period. Using a mix of Oral Language, Texel Level and Combined. Also use reciprocal teaching in my day role. Have adapted the idioms and graphic organisers for special needs work. • Will help in my teacher training as able to adapt to needs of children. • Yes there are lots of useful strategies that could be applied during classroom lessons, working with small groups. Would need to discuss with teachers during planning. • I seem to be targeted to children now with comprehension problems. Future READ ME's are in the pipeline. • YES! READ ME has extended and added to my knowledge and skills as a teaching assistant. Developed more of an awareness of reading and comprehension issues. • Absolutely – I now have a new job doing just intervention across the school and the skills I have acquired through this project have helped me and the children • Yes – much better at time management now!
Will you be involved in training other members of staff in your school in the components of oral language and comprehension intervention? If so would you like any support from the research team? Yes -36% Possibly -18% Don't know -36%	• Headmaster is keen to use the final product and I would be involved in this • I don't think so • Would be willing to if school wanted to • Yes and Yes! Would probably benefit from a 'refresher' session before I train others

Figure 8.4   (*continued*)

research team; rather they were designed to be completed with the teaching assistant and sent home to parents to promote home–school links.

PARENTS' FEEDBACK

Questionnaires were also sent to the parents of all 160 participating children at the end of the project. Figure 8.6 shows the format of the questionnaire, which invited open-ended responses as well as responses on rating scales.

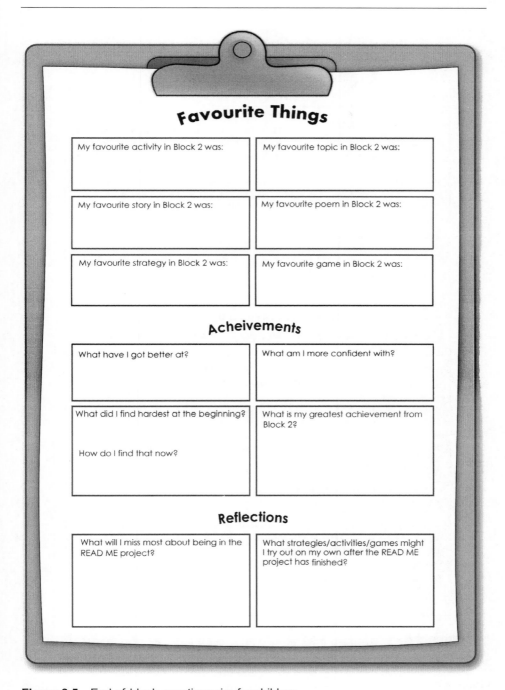

Favourite Things

My favourite activity in Block 2 was:

My favourite topic in Block 2 was:

My favourite story in Block 2 was:

My favourite poem in Block 2 was:

My favourite strategy in Block 2 was:

My favourite game in Block 2 was:

Acheivements

What have I got better at?

What am I more confident with?

What did I find hardest at the beginning?

How do I find that now?

What is my greatest achievement from Block 2?

Reflections

What will I miss most about being in the READ ME project?

What strategies/activities/games might I try out on my own after the READ ME project has finished?

Figure 8.5   End of block questionnaire for children

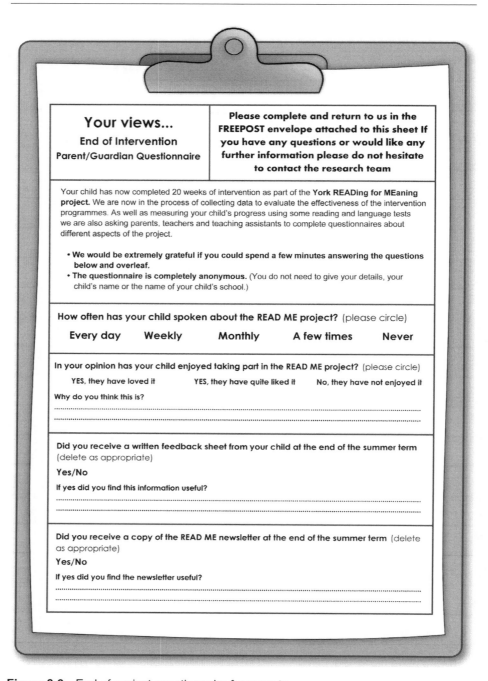

Figure 8.6   End of project questionnaire for parents

Have you looked at the READing for MEaning webpage (delete as appropriate)

Yes/No

If yes did you find the web page useful?

....
....

Since starting the READ ME project in May 2007 how would you rate your child's progress in the following areas:

	Excellent	Good	Average	Poor	Don't know
Reading aloud					
Understanding text					
Writing					
Spelling					
Maths					
Memory					
Listening					
Speaking					

Any comments/observations?

....
....

Since starting the READ ME project in May 2007 how would you rate your child's progress in the following areas:

Your child's...	Positive changes	Negative changes	No change	Don't know
Confidence				
Self esteem				
Attitude towards reading				
Motivation to do homework				
Motivation to go to school				

Any comments/observations?

....
....

Figure 8.6   (*continued*)

Thirty-four (28.33%) parental questionnaires were returned and although this was a relatively small sample, the responses provided a useful indicator of parents' perspectives. The key findings are summarised as a series of pie charts (Figures 8.7 to 8.13).

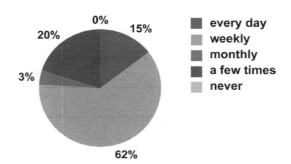

Figure 8.7 How often has your child spoken about the READ ME project?

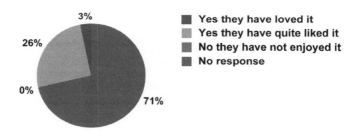

Figure 8.8 Has your child enjoyed taking part in the READ ME project?

Figure 8.7 shows that all children spoke to their parents about the READ ME project at some point and the majority of the children spoke about it regularly (at least weekly).

Figure 8.8 shows that the majority of the children either loved or quite liked taking part in the READ ME project. One parent did not respond to this question. As there was no 'don't know' option for this question it is possible that they left the question blank as they were not sure how their children felt about the project.

With regard to reading aloud, it can be seen in Figure 8.9 that a large percentage of parents reported that their children were making excellent progress in this area. A similar percentage of parents reported good progress and the remaining parents all reported average progress.

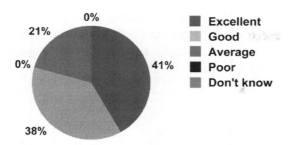

Figure 8.9 Since starting the READ ME project how would you rate your child's progress in reading aloud?

In terms of listening skills, you can see from Figure 8.10 that the majority of parents reported that their children were making good progress. A similar number of parents reported excellent and average progress and a very small percentage responded 'poor' or 'don't know'.

You can see from Figure 8.11 that 88% of parents reported that their child had made either good or excellent progress in understanding text since being involved in the project; 12% of parents reported average progress and no parents reported poor or unknown progress.

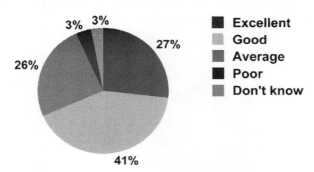

Figure 8.10 Since starting the READ ME project how would you rate your child's progress in listening?

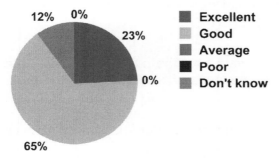

Figure 8.11 Since starting the READ ME project how would you rate your child's progress in understanding text?

You can see from Figure 8.12 that just over two-thirds of parents noted positive changes in their children's confidence since being part of the project. The remaining parents mostly reported no change and one parent reported a negative change.

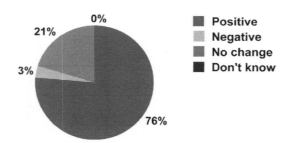

Figure 8.12   Since starting the READ ME project have you noticed any changes in your child's confidence?

With regards to attitude towards reading, you can see from Figure 8.13 that just under two-thirds of parents reported a positive change and just over a third reported no change. No parents reported a negative change and one parent responded 'don't know'.

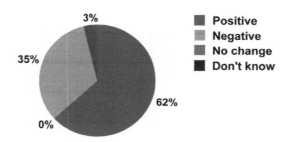

Figure 8.13   Since starting the READ ME project have you noticed any changes in your child's attitude towards reading?

In addition to the data from the rating scales, here are some sample quotes to illustrate the types of responses that the parents gave to the open questions:

- 'It has given him a thirst for learning – he is much more enthusiastic than last year.'
- 'He has enjoyed learning the meaning of new words and testing my understanding of them.'

- 'It has been a pleasure to see her grow in confidence – she has read more at home for pleasure.'
- 'This project has increased her awareness – she has been talkative about what's been happening – she questions more and opens conversations.'
- 'She has improved so much in her school work and enjoys all the learning that is given to her – I think the whole course has been very worthwhile.'
- 'Sometimes the things she has learnt pop up in conversation – she makes a connection.'
- 'I think it was an excellent and enjoyable project for my daughter.'

SUMMARY

In general the feedback data have shown that the project was well received by teaching assistants and parents, and benefits for the teaching assistants and the participating children have been highlighted. From our perspective it was noticeable that the teaching assistants became increasingly confident over the course of the first 10 weeks of intervention and once the structure and the rhythm of the intervention had become established they began to take real ownership over session planning and tailoring activities to suit individual children.

The teaching assistant's feedback, insight and ideas brought to us at the fortnightly tutorials was invaluable and was undoubtedly instrumental to the overall success of the project. Some of the challenges involved in running the project in school have been reported, one of the key issues being lack of time and having too much planned for some sessions. We responded to this as best we could whilst the project was running, for example by choosing shorter passages and developing activities that could easily be shortened or extended depending on time constraints.

Chapter 9

Theoretical and Practical Implications

In recent years there has been increased recognition of the needs of children who have difficulties in understanding what they read despite good skills in reading out loud. Research has developed our understanding of this poor comprehender profile but there remains much to do to translate theory into practice. Most previous intervention research with this group of children has been relatively small in scale, focusing on single components with teaching often delivered by researchers. Important questions about how best to support children effectively in schools remained unanswered. The *York Reading for Meaning Project* addressed this gap in practice and in the research literature.

Our project was the first Randomised Controlled Trial to evaluate methods for improving the reading comprehension skills of children with the poor comprehender profile. We hope that this book will contribute to the growing recognition that Randomised Controlled Trials are practicable and that they can provide powerful evidence concerning educational interventions.

So far we have described in detail the methods and findings of the study, the teaching materials and the practicalities of running the project. In this final chapter we stand back from the details and reflect on the practical and theoretical implications of the study.

Developing Reading Comprehension, First Edition. Paula J. Clarke, Emma Truelove, Charles Hulme and Margaret J. Snowling.
© 2014 John Wiley & Sons, Ltd. Published 2014 by John Wiley & Sons, Ltd.

HELPING CHILDREN WITH READING COMPREHENSION DIFFICULTIES

The results of the *York Reading for Meaning Project* show that once children have been identified as having reading comprehension difficulties, it is possible to provide additional teaching that can significantly improve their reading and language comprehension skills. In our study we compared the effects of three different interventions: an Oral Language programme, a Text Level programme and a Combined programme. All three programmes produced reliable gains in reading comprehension scores at the end of the 20-week teaching period and after an 11-month follow-up. However, rather strikingly, at the follow-up assessment, children who received the Oral Language programme not only maintained the improvements they made directly after the intervention but went on to make further gains in reading comprehension.

Increases in skills following the withdrawal of an intervention are highly unusual. We believe (though we cannot prove) that this pattern suggests that the Oral Language programme brought about some general and durable changes in children's approaches to language learning. In the Oral Language programme, we based our vocabulary teaching on the multiple context learning approach (Beck, McKeown and Kucan, 2002), which aims to foster an awareness of words and the ways in which they can be learnt, remembered and connected to other words and prior experiences. The multiple context learning approach is therefore highly metacognitive and we speculate that the word learning strategies at the heart of this approach may provide some explanation for the ongoing improvements in reading comprehension found in this group. Given that vocabulary is key to reading comprehension, it seems reasonable to suggest that developing the ability to use these strategies independently when encountering new words was instrumental in bringing about the long-term gains in reading comprehension that we found. A priority for research is to conduct more long-term studies of the effects of oral language teaching on reading comprehension to assess these ideas.

The Simple View of Reading (Gough and Tunmer, 1986) proposes that for successful reading for meaning, children require good decoding skills alongside well-developed language comprehension skills. The findings of our study are consistent with this model as we found that a programme that focused on spoken language was successful in supporting reading for meaning in children aged 8–10 years. An implication of the model, and of our findings, is that children's reading comprehension can and should be supported through activities to promote language comprehension alongside decoding skills. A priority for theory and practice is to establish methods for supporting these skills as early as possible in development. A preventative approach to intervention would seek to reduce the likelihood of discrepant profiles, such as the poor comprehender profile, emerging over time.

SUPPORTING CHILDREN'S LANGUAGE AS A FOUNDATION FOR READING COMPREHENSION

Recent studies have assessed children's language skills before they have learned to read, or at least in the very early stages of learning to read. Nation and colleagues (2010) showed that weaknesses in language comprehension before or just after beginning to learn to read are highly predictive of later problems with reading comprehension. Longitudinal studies are important because they suggest that early weaknesses in language (for example weaknesses in vocabulary knowledge, grammatical skills and listening comprehension) cause later difficulties in reading comprehension.

We argue that there is a pressing need for interventions that support language comprehension from the outset of reading instruction, that is at a time when the focus is typically on phonics instruction. In some recent work, we have shown that training oral language skills during the transition between preschool and the early school years can not only improve vocabulary, listening comprehension and narrative skills but also has a positive effect on the development of reading comprehension some six months later (Fricke *et al.*, 2013). Furthermore, in this study we found that gains in reading comprehension were mediated by improvements in oral language over and above the effects of decoding. These findings underline the Simple View of Reading and reinforce the findings of the study presented in this book; moreover, they suggest that an intervention which focuses on teaching similar components to those taught in the *York Reading for Meaning Project*'s Oral Language programme can be delivered early in a child's schooling to provide a better foundation for reading comprehension.

FEATURES OF SUCCESSFUL TEACHING APPROACHES

The teaching principles that underpinned the intervention sessions and activities in the *York Reading for Meaning Project* are well established. We drew on Vygotskian notions and embedded our approaches within the framework of cooperative learning. Based on feedback from teaching assistants and our own observations of the intervention sessions, we feel that peer learning was a key feature that contributed to the success of the programmes. Peer learning was particularly important for those activities in which multiple perspectives were needed to develop rich representations of language and text, for example multiple context vocabulary learning and reciprocal teaching. In the *York Reading for Meaning Project*, interventions were largely delivered to pairs of children; however, we feel that our activities could easily be adapted for small group and class-based teaching.

> **Box 9.1**   TA commentary
>
> Most of the skills that the children learned were easily transferable into the whole class guided reading sessions, and once they realised that they were already able to summarise, illustrate, clarify and question they were leading their small reading groups in these activities. This was a real boost to their confidence and had acted as a great pre-teaching activity.

The 'little and often' (or distributed practice) approach to intervention and teaching shaped the design of our intervention approaches. It is well established that children learn most effectively through short activities that build up over time (see Seabrook, Brown and Solity, 2005). In our interventions we carefully constructed the sessions around a routine timetable involving short components that linked together in 30-minute sessions. We feel that children really benefited from opportunities to revisit and consolidate knowledge and strategy use over an extended period of time. We would recommend that short components are linked through common themes and passages to ensure sessions do not become disjointed. Feedback from teaching assistants presented informally during tutorials suggested that some components were more suited to short activities than others; for example, they reported that inferencing activities would have benefited from more time to engage with the material in depth whereas components such as vocabulary and figurative language lent themselves particularly well to brief inputs.

To meet our theoretical objectives, and as a condition of the Randomised Controlled Trial design of the research, it was essential for us to provide comprehensive manuals that supported teaching assistants to deliver the intervention programmes consistently across schools. In considering the future implications of the *York Reading for Meaning Project*, we acknowledge that many schools may not be able to deliver 20-week intervention using exactly the same passages and materials utilised in our project. Although our evidence only allows us to make claims about the interventions we delivered during the project, one of the motivations for writing this book was to share effective approaches and assist practitioners in developing methods of supporting children with reading comprehension difficulties. To enable widespread application of these approaches, it may be that a more flexible approach would be desirable. In this way, practitioners could tailor approaches to their particular context and the needs of the children they are supporting.

IDENTIFYING CHILDREN WITH READING COMPREHENSION DIFFICULTIES

It is clear that problems in mastering reading comprehension skills are quite common. We also believe that such problems often go unnoticed in the classroom. In the *York Reading for Meaning Project* 84 children out of 1120 (7.5%) who were screened were classified as having a specific difficulty with reading comprehension (defined as a reading comprehension score on the Neale Analysis of Reading Ability that was 1 standard deviation below their reading fluency as assessed by the Test of Word Reading Efficiency). Such a finding suggests that a weakness in reading comprehension skills in relation to word reading skills is relatively common. However, one might object that a discrepancy definition of this sort identifies children whose absolute levels of reading comprehension are not a serious concern. Indeed, some of the children in our sample had reading comprehension skills that were comfortably in the average range; it was just that their reading comprehension scores fell below the level expected given their very good word reading skills.

Better evidence about how common the poor comprehender profile is comes from data that were collected during the standardization of a reading test in the United Kingdom (the York Assessment of Reading for Comprehension; Snowling *et al.*, 2009). The standardization of this test was conducted using a representative sample of 1324 UK primary school children. Of this sample, 10.3% achieved a reading comprehension score that was substantially below their reading accuracy score (by more than 1 standard deviation). This figure is actually higher than the 7.5% we found in the *York Reading for Meaning Project*, but once again this figure includes some children with average to good reading comprehension skills who have exceptionally good decoding skills. To identify children with the poor comprehender profile who have more pronounced educational needs, we can select those children whose reading comprehension scores are equal to or below a standard score of 90 and whose reading accuracy scores are at a standard score of 90 or above (where a standard score of 100 is average and scores between 85 and 115 fall within the average range). Arguably, this is quite a stringent set of criteria, which identifies children whose reading comprehension abilities are lower than we would expect for their age. In the standardisation sample, 3.3% of children of primary school aged children met this criterion and could be considered particularly in need of support with developing reading comprehension skills. Interestingly, 28% of these children spoke English as an additional language, compared to 14% of the rest of the sample (see also Lervåg and Aukrust, 2010, for similar data from a sample of children in Norway). These findings suggest that many children whose first language is not English might require and benefit from support with reading comprehension.

We suggest that identifying children with the poor comprehender profile is both important and achievable for practitioners. Teachers and educational professionals can do this by measuring children's reading accuracy and reading comprehension skills and considering the discrepancy between the two abilities alongside the levels at which the child is working. Standardised tests such as the York Assessment of Reading for Comprehension (Snowling *et al.*, 2009) provide a way of doing this. With this information, practitioners can plan to meet the comprehension needs of children displaying this profile by drawing on the evidence-based approaches discussed throughout this book.

SUMMARY

The *York Reading for Meaning Project* produced quite striking results in relation to how best to help children with difficulties in understanding what they read. The Oral Language programme in particular appears to be a highly successful intervention with durable and potentially wide-ranging benefits. We hope that the information in this book has provided an informative, evidence-based starting point from which to develop approaches to supporting reading comprehension in both research and practice.

Summary Points

- Reading comprehension problems are common but often 'hidden' behind strong decoding skills.
- Gains in vocabulary knowledge appear to be critical in helping to bring about improvements in reading comprehension.
- Weak oral language skills are one of the main contributors to reading comprehension difficulties.
- Developing literacy skills depends critically upon oral language skills. It is important that school systems recognise this and work to improve the language skills of children who enter school with language learning difficulties.
- Trained teaching assistants can be supported to deliver interventions that foster reading comprehension and are valuable members of the language and literacy support team.

We hope that the content of this book will inspire practitioners to:

- Identify the needs of children with reading comprehension difficulties.
- Reflect on their current practice and existing resources within their contexts.
- Consider ways in which they could support comprehension needs.
- Monitor and evaluate progress in response to teaching.
- Raise awareness of the importance of supporting language comprehension and the implications for literacy development.

Appendices

APPENDIX 1. CONSENT PROCEDURES

The project was approved by the Research Ethics Committee of the Department of Psychology, University of York, and was conducted in accordance with British Psychological Society (BPS) guidance.

Initial group screening was carried out with head teacher's permission. No children were singled out or worked with individually at this stage and it was felt that the assessments did not deviate significantly from everyday school activities.

At the point at which children were identified to take part in the individual screening phase, parents received information letters and consent forms. The research team and key members of school staff were on hand at this stage to respond to parent enquiries and explain the project orally where necessary. Only after we had received a signed consent form from the parents were the children the considered to be recruited to the study.

The children were also asked before each assessment to give their assent and were reassured that they could discontinue or withdraw from the study at any point without consequence. The study was introduced as a project for children who were doing very well with reading words and so was framed in a way that emphasised the children's strengths. We explained that the focus was on helping children to develop an understanding of what the books they were reading were all about. We reinforced our belief that involvement in the project should help the children to read, enjoy and understand a greater range of books in the future.

Developing Reading Comprehension, First Edition. Paula J. Clarke, Emma Truelove, Charles Hulme and Margaret J. Snowling.
© 2014 John Wiley & Sons, Ltd. Published 2014 by John Wiley & Sons, Ltd.

APPENDIX 2. TRAINING OF TEACHING ASSISTANTS

Teaching assistants were invited to an initial training course, which took place over two and a half days at the University. The training was compulsory and fully funded. Class teachers were also invited to the first day but unfortunately only a small number of teachers were able to attend. The training covered the following key areas:

- The aims of the project
- What is reading comprehension and why is it important?
- Overview of the design of the project
- Details of selection and assessment procedures
- Administration of pre-test measures.
- Key teaching techniques (scaffolding, modelling, etc.)
- The Oral Language programme – rationale and components
- The Text Level programme – rationale and components
- The Combined programme – rationale and components
- Treatment fidelity
- House keeping.

The content was delivered in a variety of different ways including lecture style sessions, small group work, pair discussions and role play. Emphasis was placed on creating a warm supportive environment in which attendees could share ideas, experiences and opinions. The teaching assistants were encouraged to build a community and support network between one another. From the start, we were keen to establish a strong partnership between ourselves (the research team) and the group of teaching assistants to allow us to develop the project together. We wanted to dispel the idea that as researchers we were the experts; rather, we talked about the knowledge and the expertise that we all brought to the table and the value of bringing together a variety of perspectives from theory and practice. The breaking down of perceived boundaries between researchers and teaching assistants was considered vital to the success of the project.

APPENDIX 3. TEACHING ASSISTANT FEEDBACK ON TRAINING

Following the training we invited the teaching assistants to provide us with feedback. Using a written questionnaire we asked: (1) What have

What have you found useful this week?

- Meeting other schools involved
- Role play
- Demonstrations
- Video clips
- Background information
- Understanding how the programme works and its purpose.
- Going through all three programmes separately
- Reassurance that everyone else was finding it hard at first
- Having everything written down word for word
- Knowing that help is on the end of the phone
- A friendly, relaxed atmosphere
- Colour coded sessions/worksheets/resources

"To realise that others have the same worries, concerns and gripes (!) as me"

"Role play - observing & taking part. It made it all seem more real and doable."

What would you like to cover in more depth in the fortnightly tutorials?

- Things as and when they come up
- Managing time
- Feedback about the progress of the project

"To be honest I'm not sure yet as I think I'll know more once I've started the programme with the children. There may be a need to cover timing of the sessions as this will probably be the hardest part for me."

Do you have any comments about the contents of the programmes/manuals/resources etc.

- Very well laid out
- Virtually idiot proof
- Well structured yet flexible
- Self explanatory
- General resources list would be useful

"Clearly laid out session scripts with references to resources easy to follow - but would prefer order of session sections to be laid out in order used - not backwards and forwards to reading passages"

"A lot of work to fit into each session/week. Some very technical language in explanations about programme."

"The manual is well written and easy to understand. I have no worries at the moment about delivering this intervention."

Any general comments?

"It has been a thoroughly enjoyable few days and I look forward to meeting up with others on the programme at the tutorials. Very excited about how it will all unfold."

"Very friendly atmosphere. Well fed and watered!"

"The project is everything I had hoped it would be - challenging, exciting, ground breaking (is that too big a word?). I hope I continue to feel the same... and thank you!"

"Can't wait to "get my teeth into it" (see! using idioms already !)

Figure A.1 Teaching assistant feedback following training

you found useful this week? (2) What would you like to cover in more depth in the fortnightly tutorials? (3) Do you have any comments about the content of the programmes/manuals/resources, etc.? (4) Any general comments? Figure A.1 is a summary of the feedback we received with some representative quotes.

APPENDIX 4. MANUAL PRODUCTION

The manual was designed to provide highly detailed 'model' sessions for the teaching assistants to use as a guide when delivering the programmes. The Oral Language programme manual was split into three parts: (1) session plans, (2) resources, (3) worksheets; the Text Level and Combined programme manuals comprised these as well as a further part: (4) a reader. As all teaching assistants delivered all intervention programmes, the manuals were fully coloured coded to reduce confusion and aid organisation.

The manual was produced and released in parts. During the initial training the TAs received four weeks of teaching material for each of the programmes. At each subsequent tutorial two further weeks of material was made available. Although this way of producing material placed the team under considerable pressure of time, it allowed us to respond quickly to the feedback we were receiving from the TAs about the programmes and to incorporate changes rapidly. The manuals that were produced were therefore tailored to the children and refined according to suggestions coming through from practice.

The manual was designed to be user-friendly with sections highlighting the components to be taught, the objectives for the session and the equipment needed. It was fully scripted with key directive words such as **explain**, **say**, **ask**, **discuss** highlighted in bold. All resources, worksheets and reader pages were carefully numbered to aid navigation through the programmes. Sample sections from the manual for each programme are provided throughout Chapters 5, 6 and 7.

APPENDIX 5. ADDITIONAL PREPARATION

Whilst every effort was made to provide a comprehensive set of materials, some extra preparation was required each week. Teaching assistants received funding for this preparation time with an allowance of two hours per week. Feedback from teaching assistants indicated that in reality they tended to use more time than this allowance and we regularly provided advice on how to streamline some of the additional work. The main things that the teaching assistants needed to do in preparation are listed below:

- Read through the session plans.
- Revisit record sheets from the previous week to inform session planning.
- Photocopy worksheets and readers.
- Prepare games (e.g. spinners, dice, mystery bags, etc.).
- Prepare general resources (e.g. wall posters, children's folders, story mountain, etc.).
- Laminate core resources (optional).

APPENDIX 6. FORTNIGHTLY TUTORIAL GROUPS

The content of the tutorial group sessions varied across the project depending on the immediate needs of the groups. Broadly speaking, the sessions lasted approximately two hours and contained:

1. Refreshments and informal catch-up
2. Sharing of experiences from the previous two weeks of intervention
3. Opportunities to highlight possible changes in future versions of the activities
4. Suggestions for other activities to include
5. Discussion of any particular issues relating to the individual or pairs of children
6. Collecting completed record sheets
7. Time to revise and work on specific components (as needed)
8. Collective read through of next two weeks of intervention
9. Role play or demonstration of any new activities
10. Time for questions.

APPENDIX 7. RECORD SHEETS

For each session the teaching assistants were required to complete a record sheet. Record sheets provided a space to keep track of attendance, children's progress, success of activities, time taken to complete each activity, any ideas for future sessions and points of feedback for the research team. Record sheets provided another channel of communication between us (the research team) and the teaching assistants.

READ ME Project Record Sheet

School: _____ Teaching Assistant: _____			
Date:_____ Week:_____	TL☐ COM☐ OL☐	Group Session: _____	Individual Session: _____
Activity 1:	Activity 2:	Activity 3:	Activity 4:
Feedback:			

APPENDIX 8. OBSERVATIONS AND ON-SITE FEEDBACK

Each TA was observed by a member of the research team four times at regular intervals during the interventions. This was a vital part of the training and monitoring of intervention delivery. From the perspective of the research team, we needed to establish whether the programmes were being delivered in the way in which we intended and to gain a picture of the extent to which delivery was consistent across schools. We used a structured observation schedule (see Figure A.2) to record the observations and made notes highlighting examples of best practice and areas for development. We rated each part of the session using the following scoring system: 3 (good, could be used as a model of best practice), 2 (satisfactory), 1 (poor – some development required). The amount of time used for each section and activity was noted as well as instances in which an activity was not working or being administered incorrectly. Notes regarding the general behaviour of the group/individual and how the teaching assistants dealt with any difficult behaviour were made. Further key points that the observers looked out for were:

York Reading for Meaning Project – Observation Checklist

School_____ Date_____ Session No_____

Pair or Individual_____ Attendance_____

Section/Activity	3	2	1	Observed yes/no
Organisation				
Planning				
Introduction				
notes				
TIME TAKEN:				
1._____				
notes				
TIME TAKEN:				
2._____				
notes				
TIME TAKEN:				
3._____				
notes				
TIME TAKEN:				
4._____				
notes				
TIME TAKEN:				
(Combined programme only)				
5._____				
notes				
TIME TAKEN:				
Plenary				
notes				
TIME TAKEN:				
General:				
Listening rules used				
Clear instructions given				
Appropriate wait times				
Simple use of language				

Figure A.2 Observation checklist

a. Is the programme aimed at the correct level for each child?
b. How user-friendly does the programme appear to be?
c. Do the children seem to enjoy the programme?
d. Are the children engaged in the session?

e. Do the sessions run smoothly?
f. Are the timings realistic for each programme, that is are teaching assistants managing to get through the whole session in the allotted time? Are the approximate times allocated to each section of a session (i) realistic and (ii) being adhered to?
g. Environmental issues, that is what is the room like, how much space does the teaching assistant have for running group sessions? Is the room too hot/cold?

During the sessions the children were reassured that we were not there to observe them but rather to watch their teaching assistant and find out about all the different things they were doing in their sessions. We made every effort to be as unobtrusive as possible during our observations. Immediately following each observation we discussed the session with the teaching assistant. We were mindful of maintaining a warm, collaborative relationship with the teaching assistants and tried to ensure that they did not feel like they were being assessed or judged. We reinforced the idea that we were all learning and developing the programmes together and that observations gave us all a good opportunity to reflect on the relative successes and difficulties in the design and delivery of the activities. Whilst initially perceived as daunting, over time the teaching assistants became increasingly relaxed about observations.

We also provided general feedback to all the teaching assistants after each set of observations had been completed. Figure A.3 is a summary of the feedback we provided after the first set of observations; this was delivered orally using the bullet points listed as prompts.

APPENDIX 9. NEWSLETTERS

The research team produced newsletters to go out to the schools and the parents. Each school was sent copies to distribute in their staff room and to go home with the children involved in the project in their school bags. These gave general information about the project as well as specific details of the texts, topics and strategies that were being focused on in the sessions. Each newsletter also included a timeline to show the progress of the project and highlight forthcoming phases.

APPENDIX 10. SHARING DATA

The schools received two feedback reports containing the general results of the study and the individual data from the children in their school.

Observation Feedback – Block 1

• Thank you for the warm welcome.

• It was a great privilege to observe, we were very impressed and found the experience stimulating.

• How was the experience for you?

• How was the experience for the children?

We liked:

• **Commitment:** Time, energy, preparation, organisation of the three programmes

• **Children:** Motivated, positive self esteem, enthusiastic, 'have a go' attitude, developing ideas (particularly with regards story planning), confidence linked to the routine, verbalising of strategies, recall of previous sessions, spontaneous use of idioms and vocabulary and developing peer collaboration

• **Relationship between TAs and children:** Positive, encouraging, good eye contact, appropriate body language, use of humour, sensitive to different personalities and abilities, firm but gentle management, tailoring approaches to individuals strengths and weaknesses, creation of new storyboards to match individual children's interests

• **Organisation:** Quality of materials prepared for each session, storage, labelling, highlighting of text to read, children's folders, excellent display boards

• **Timing:** On the whole excellent, emphasis on the right things, keeping the key concepts and content

• **Programme delivery:** Use of voice for emphasis, pauses and wait times, clear instructions, reinforcement of technical language relating to the strategies, 'little and often' exposure to vocabulary and idioms, relating vocabulary to idioms and children's experiences, monitoring of children's understanding, consistent use of strategies, reminders of listening rules, reading aloud with children and encouraging pointing to words, careful pronunciation of words, encouraging children to verbalise, some evidence of flexibility and deviation from the script, some evidence of personalising the programme

• **Rewards:** Varied use of certificates and stickers, clear reasons for rewards provided

Reminders:

• Find time to **liaise** with Year 4 teachers

• **Look ahead** and find out about any changes to school timetable

• **Oral Language programme** – the teaching assistant should read the text not the child – please do not give the child the passage

• Encourage the children to **verbalise strategies** using an audible voice

• **Rewards** – give reasons, vary the reasons and encourage the children to self monitor their own responses and each others

• **Working from the manual** – freedom to deviate from the script, don't be afraid to add your own personality and thoughts

• **Today we are going to...** – write on, point to, read aloud and refer to during the session and in the plenary (it is nice to see that children are becoming involved in this process and are learning what to expect from a session, as the programme progresses this should become quite automatic and quick)

• **Name each activity** – Explain "Now we are going to..." encourage children to recall and verbalise the activities to help build the routine

• **Enjoy!!**

Figure A.3 Summary of the feedback given to the teaching assistants following observations

These went directly to the head teachers and it was their responsibility to pass the data on to the teaching assistants, class teachers and children's parents. One report was released after the results were collated immediately following the intervention and another report detailed the results when children were re-tested 11 months later. Care was taken to ensure that a member of the research team met with the head teacher to talk through the results and this facilitated discussion around the impact of the research, perceptions and experiences of the school and feedback concerning how the work might be taken forward in the future.

Glossary

Active listening. A method of listening that focuses on understanding the content of what the speaker is saying as well as the intent behind the words. The listener is encouraged to feed back what they hear to the speaker, in ways such as paraphrasing or re-stating, to confirm their understanding.

Antonym. A word whose meaning is opposite to that of another word.

Assessment. The use of bespoke and standardized tests and questionnaires to measure an individual's knowledge and abilities.

Attrition. The loss of participants from a study over time. If attrition does not occur randomly (i.e. the reason for dropping out is related to the factors being studied) it can bias the outcome of a trial.

Baseline data. Initial test data that are collected prior to the commencement of an intervention programme so that it can subsequently be compared with data gathered after the programme in order to assess the impact of the intervention.

Behavioural manifestation. The manner in which underlying cognitive impairments/difficulties present themselves in the behaviour of an individual.

Blinding. The practice of ensuring that those assessing changes in behaviour of the participants are unaware of which intervention has been received so that they will not inadvertently bias the results.

Causality. The relationship between an event (the cause) and a second event (the effect), where the second event is understood as a consequence of the first.

Developing Reading Comprehension, First Edition. Paula J. Clarke, Emma Truelove,
Charles Hulme and Margaret J. Snowling.
© 2014 John Wiley & Sons, Ltd. Published 2014 by John Wiley & Sons, Ltd.

Chronological age match. A case control research strategy in which a group of clinical cases are compared to a group of typically developing children of the same chronological age.

Clarification. To remove uncertainty or confusion when comprehension has broken down, e.g. asking a teacher what a word means when it is not understood.

Cognitive resources. The mental capacities available to an individual to allocate to any given task.

Collective understanding. A richer, group knowledge of the meaning of a passage or activity achieved through discussion of each group member's interpretation and ideas.

Comprehension. The ability to understand and gain meaning from what has been heard or read.

Comprehension age match. Following the logic of the reading-level match design, the comprehension age match design has been used to investigate underlying factors contributing to reading comprehension impairments. Children with poor comprehension are matched to younger children who score at the same level on a comprehension test. If poor comprehenders show an impairment in a particular cognitive or linguistic skill relative to comprehension age controls, that skill is unlikely to be a simple consequence of comprehension level.

Comprehension monitoring. The ability to recognise when your own comprehension of a text has broken down.

CONSORT. This is an abbreviation of Consolidated Standards of Reporting Trials, a set of recommendations for reporting Randomized Controlled Trials.

Construction-integration model. A model proposed by Kintsch and Rawson (2005), which suggests that when an individual reads a text, they create a personal representation of its meaning made up of their own general knowledge and the information from the text itself. The processes involved in deciphering the text are described according to three levels: the linguistic level, the microstructure and the macrostructure. Together these form what is called a 'textbase'. The textbase combines with the reader's existing general knowledge to form a personal representation of the meaning of the text. This interpretation is called the situation model.

Control group. A subgroup of the sample in an RCT who do not receive the intervention being evaluated. Control groups may receive no intervention or may receive an alternative intervention that is considered unlikely to improve the skills targeted by the intervention that is being evaluated (e.g. giving music lessons rather that a reading intervention, when evaluating how to improve reading skills). The use of a control group is necessary to rule out the possibility that gains would have been made regardless of whether or not a specific intervention had been implemented.

Control task. A task designed to monitor performance on measures unrelated to the intervention activities so that changes in performance due to factors unrelated to the intervention methods can be disentangled from any effects that were due to the intervention itself. Should it be found that participants improve not only on measures related (e.g. one-on-one attention from a teacher) to the intervention but also on the control task, it would not be possible to conclude that the intervention had specific effects.

Criteria for inclusion. A set of conditions that a participant must meet before they can be included as a participant in the study.

Cut-off. The point at which an individual's scores on assessment measures will deem them to be diagnosed with a specific disorder.

Decoding. The use of strategies to decipher printed words so that they can be pronounced.

Distributed practice. A method of learning where students participate in study sessions that are relatively short with intervals in between each study session. This contrasts with Massed Practice which involves long study sessions. There is evidence that Distributed Practice leads to better learning than Massed Practice.

Dyslexia. A specific learning disability characterised by severe difficulties in learning to read and spell.

Early indicators. Signs prior to the diagnosis of a disorder that suggest an individual will develop it in the future.

English as an additional language (EAL). Individuals who speak English as a second language.

Error detection task. A test where the participant's aim is to detect something that is wrong, e.g. which word in a sentence is spelled incorrectly.

Figurative language. Words or phrases that are not literal, or mean something other than what they first appear to. Similes and metaphors are two common examples of figurative language.

Fluency. The ability to read text smoothly and quickly.

Generalisability. The extent to which a study's findings can be extended to apply to natural settings (i.e. in normal classroom/learning situations).

Global level. In relation to text comprehension, a coherent understanding of the whole text, such as ideas about its theme, point, moral, etc.,

Grammar. The way words and word parts are combined to convey different meanings.

Hawthorne effect. A non-specific improvement resulting from children receiving extra attention. Merely participating in a study where teachers and children believe they will benefit can improve performance. We need to distinguish such general improvements (Hawthorne effects) from specific effects of a teaching programme.

Hypothesis. A testable prediction about the relationship between at least two variables.

Idiom. A phrase or expression established by popular usage as having a meaning that is not deducible from the individual words that make it up, e.g. having a chip on your shoulder.

Individualisation. Tailoring a programme to an individual's specific needs.

Inference. Drawing a conclusion from incomplete information.

Constructive inference. An inference that is required in order to integrate different sources of information, such as information from a text and general knowledge.

Elaborative inference. An inference that is not necessary to establish cohesion in a text, but serves to enrich a reader's representation of the text. Such inferences may help a reader or listener to build a full mental model of an event or situation.

Intonation. The rise and fall of the voice during speech.

Language profile. A summary of an individual's language abilities, delineating their strengths and weaknesses in different skills required to use and understand language, e.g. vocabulary.

Language skills. An individual's level of language competence. Language skills can be classified as reflecting four domains of language: phonology, semantics, grammar and pragmatics.

Liaison group. A group of lay and professional people (e.g. educational psychologists or specialist teachers) who have knowledge about the area of research being studied and who provide feedback and advice on how best to design a study.

Linguistic level. The cognitive level at which the reader recognises and processes individual words and their meanings.

Listening comprehension. The ability to understand a spoken narrative; sometimes contrasted with Reading Comprehension – the ability to understand written text.

Literal comprehension. A level of understanding that reflects surface details of a text. Often it is important to achieve a 'deeper level' of comprehension – the reader should understand not only the events in a story but the effects of those events on the characters' emotions and actions.

Longitudinal study. A study where participants are assessed repeatedly over a period of time.

Macrostructure. The global conceptual structure of a text; a representation of the interrelationships between the higher-order topics or units of microstructure.

Maintenance assessment. An assessment conducted a length of time after the intervention has come to an end to examine whether changes or improvements in participant performance due to the intervention have remained or changed over time.

Manualised intervention. An intervention that has a specific structure that can be outlined in a manual.

Massed practice. A method of learning where students participate in only a few study sessions that are long (cf. distributed practice).

Matthew effect. A term adopted to describe how early achievement fosters subsequent achievements. For example, the consequences of reading success or failure: children who are reading well experience more print, acquire more vocabulary and develop even stronger reading skills; conversely, children who are poor readers read less, fail to develop knowledge and vocabulary, which inhibits further growth in reading.

Mechanics of reading. The basic skills required for reading, e.g. decoding skills.

Mediator. Mediators are variables that explain the effects of one thing on another. For example, changes in DNA caused by cigarette smoke may mediate (provide an explanation for) the effects of cigarette smoking on rates of lung cancer. In the study reported here vocabulary knowledge is a mediator of the effects of interventions on comprehension.

Mental imagery. The ability to visualise images in our minds in the absence of the original stimuli.

Mental model. An internal representation of a particular aspect of the external world; an analogue of the real world.

Metacognition. Knowledge of one's own cognitive processes and the efficient use of this self-awareness to self-regulate these cognitive processes.

Metacognitive strategies/processes. Ways of monitoring and/or improving our own learning and understanding.

Microstructure. The local conceptual structure of a text; a representation of the inter-relationships between the propositions expressed in the content of the text.

Mind map. A diagram used to visually display and link information. A central concept is linked by lines or arrows to other related concepts, which in turn are linked to other associated ideas, such that a hierarchy of related ideas is depicted.

Mnemonics. Techniques used to aid memory.

Modelling. This is a general term used to refer to the idea that adults can teach behaviours or attitudes to a child by demonstration. Whereas some modelling may be deliberate and include repeated demonstrations designed to improve the child's independent performance, other modelling and learning may occur more naturalistically in the course of daily interactions.

Multicomponential. Something composed of multiple components or parts.

Multiple context learning. Teaching vocabulary using a variety of different techniques and in many different situations to produce a fuller understanding of a word.

Narrative. A spoken or written account of connected events; a story.

Neale analysis of reading ability (NARA II). A test commonly used to measure reading accuracy, comprehension and rate. Children read short passages aloud and answer questions about the contents of each passage.

Non-phonological language difficulties. Difficulties in language skills not related to the sound structure of language – e.g. knowledge of word meanings and grammatical skills that deal with the combination of word meanings in sentences.

Non-verbal reasoning. The ability to understand information and find solutions to problems without the use of language.

Non-words (e.g. **blint).** Letter or phoneme strings that are not words in a language. Non-words are often used to assess children's decoding skills in reading.

Oral narrative. A spoken narrative or story.

Peer learning (cooperative learning). A form of learning in which students engage in teaching each other.

Phoneme. The smallest unit of speech that distinguishes meaning – the word CAT has three phonemes.

Phonic. Phonic methods (or phonics) are methods of teaching reading that focus on getting children to understand how letters in printed words map on to the phonemes in spoken words.

Phonology. The system that maps speech sounds on to meanings.

Plenary sessions. Sessions that provide a summary of material covered earlier.

Poor comprehenders. Children who, despite age-appropriate reading accuracy, are poor at understanding what they read. Poor reading comprehension usually arises in the context of more general difficulties with language comprehension.

Pragmatics. The language system concerned with the context-appropriate use of language and the ability of speakers to communicate more than that which is explicitly stated.

Prediction. A statement of what one thinks will happen. In reference to reading text, in order to sensibly predict what might happen next, a child is required to synthesise what is already known about the passage with their background knowledge about the world.

Preposition. A connecting word that depicts the relationship of a noun or pronoun to another word in the sentence, e.g. by, like, as, to, from.

Prevalence. The proportion of a population that have a disorder at any given point in time.

Question generation. A technique of encouraging a child to generate or produce questions about a passage they have encountered, with the aim of deepening their understanding of the passage by consideration of its content.

Random allocation. The random assignment of participants to the different experimental conditions in a study. This process helps to ensure that the treatment and control groups are as similar as possible prior to treatment.

Randomised controlled trial. An evaluation of a teaching method or medical treatment in which people are assigned 'at random' to either receive an intervention or to be in a control group.

Reading accuracy. The ability to read words and texts correctly, as assessed by measures of reading aloud.

Reading-age matched (RA). A research strategy used to compare children with reading impairments with younger children reading at the same level of reading skill.

Reading profile. A summary of an individual's reading highlighting their strengths and weaknesses in different component reading skills, e.g. decoding vs and comprehension.

Reading strategy. The way in which an individual approaches reading and the tools they use to help them do so.

Reciprocal teaching. An instructional activity where the teacher and student take turns leading discussions of the text in order to aid the student's understanding of its meaning. This is guided by four cognitive strategies: summarizing, question generating, clarifying and predicting.

Reliability. The consistency of a measure. A test is considered reliable if it produces the same result repeatedly.

Remedial approach. An approach that focuses on ameliorating difficulties after they have developed.

Sample. A number of participants drawn from an entire population.

Scaffolding. Adult interactions with children that aid skill or conceptual development by providing support at a level at, or just beyond, the child's current level of ability. Scaffolding allows for the adult to match the support provided to the individual needs of different children, and also allows for the gradual removal of explicit support once the child is able to independently enact the target behaviour.

Schematic representation. A diagram that represents its elements using abstract or graphic symbols.

Semantics. The aspect of language that deals with meaning.

Sentence span task. A task where the participant is presented with a series of short sentences and asked to decide if each one is true or false. At the same time, the participant is required to store (and remember) the final word from each sentence and recall these final words at the end of the task in the order they were presented.

Simile. A figure of speech that explicitly compares two unlike things, typically by employing the words 'like' or 'as'.

Simple view of reading. A theory that states that reading comprehension is the product of listening comprehension ability (language) and word reading ability (decoding).

Single strategy interventions. Interventions that focus on only one variable that could affect the outcome measure (e.g. an intervention for poor comprehension that only focused on increasing vocabulary knowledge).

Situation model. A mental model of the situation described by the text, which typically involves combining information explicitly stated in the text with prior knowledge.

Social learning theory. A theory that argues that social behaviour (any type of behaviour that we display socially) is learned primarily by observing and imitating the actions of others.

Socio-cultural theories. Theories that suggest that our society and culture (social customs, beliefs, values and language) shape our cognition (the way we think) and how we view ourselves and the world.

Socio-economic status (SES). SES is traditionally defined as the joint product of an adult's income and educational status. Some definitions of SES use a rating of adult occupation. In households or families with multiple adult residents, the higher status occupation or the highest educational achievement is typically used.

Special educational needs. A child has special educational needs if they require extra educational provision to be made for them beyond the standard curriculum.

Specific language impairment (SLI). A developmental disorder of language in which language skills are significantly below the age-appropriate level and non-verbal skills are within the normal range.

Standardised tests. Tests that are administered, scored and analysed under uniform (standardized) conditions for all people.

Standard of coherence. The degree to which an individual is concerned with whether text makes sense and what level their standard is for determining whether they have understood something they have read.

Standard scores. A way of expressing a person's performance relative to that of a given population of the same age. The average standard score is set at 100 with a standard deviation of 15. Thus, a score of 85 indicates a moderate level of difficulty (around 16% of children would score at this level or below).

Story planner. A prop for remembering, rehearsing and recording each section of a story.

Summarisation. Producing an overview of a piece of text or activity in a concise and appropriate manner.

Synonym. A word or phrase that means the same, or nearly the same, as another word in the language.

Syntax. An aspect of grammar that deals with morpheme combination and word order in sentences.

Synthesise. To combine to form a more multifaceted concept, e.g. to gain a full understanding of the text, a child must synthesise what they have read with their background knowledge about the world.

Teaching assistant (TA). A teaching assistant is an individual who assists teachers in school and provides extra support to students.

Teaching strategies. Methods a teacher can use to convey knowledge to a student and improve their overall learning, e.g. clarification, summarisation, prediction, question generation.

Test of word reading efficiency (TOWRE). A test to assess efficiency of sight word reading and phonemic decoding (non-word reading) in children and adults.

Textbase. The representation of the content of a text; the microstructure and the macrostructure together.

Text cohesion. The grammatical and lexical links within a passage of text that hold it together and give it meaning.

Text comprehension programme. An intervention programme focused on text-level processes of reading. The intervention focuses on four main areas: Metacognitive Strategies, Reciprocal Teaching with Written Language, Inferencing from Text and Written Narrative.

Text-level processes. Cognitive abilities that are directly related to the understanding of text, e.g. inferencing and comprehension monitoring.

Theory of mind. A person's ability to attribute mental states, e.g. thoughts and beliefs, to themselves and others, and the appreciation that other people's mental states may be different to their own.

'Think-aloud' activity. A reading activity in which the student is encouraged to speak their thoughts about a passage aloud in order to bring focus on to aspects of reading comprehension that could otherwise go unnoticed.

Validity. For psychological and educational tests – a measure of the extent to which a test measures what it is designed to measure.

Verbal reasoning. The ability to understand information and find solutions to problems using concepts that are framed in words.

Visual cues. Tools in the form of images or gestures (anything you can see) that make the meaning of something clearer.

Visual representation. An idea, word or object depicted using imagery, gesture or another medium that someone can see.

Vocabulary. The body of words known, used by, and understood by a particular individual.

Vygotskian principles. A term based on the work of the Russian psychologist Lev Vygotsky. These principles, developed within a social-cultural framework, emphasise the importance of social interaction in the development of cognitive skills. Vygotsky viewed learning as being socially mediated and argued that knowledge is constructed by people together, in social situations. He highlighted the importance of language as a tool in social interaction and learning and thought it was influential in transforming thinking.

Waiting list control group. A comparison group from whom treatment is withheld in a controlled trial. After the evaluation is complete, the waiting list control group receives the intervention.

Wechsler individual achievement test (WIAT-II). An assessment tool that measures an individual's academic skills and problem-solving abilities.

Working memory. A limited capacity system that supports both the maintenance and processing of information during a task.

Zone of proximal development. The difference between what a child can achieve independently and what a child can achieve with guidance and encouragement from a skilled partner or teacher.

References

Bandura, A. (1977). *Social learning theory*. Englewood Cliffs, N.J.: Prentice Hall.

Beck, I. L., & McKeown, M. G. (1981). Developing questions that promote comprehension: the story map. *Language Arts*, *58*, 913–918.

Beck, I.L., & McKeown, M. G. (1985). Teaching vocabulary: making the instruction fit the goal. *Educational Perspectives*, *23*(1), 11–15.

Beck, I. L., McKeown, M. G., & Kucan, L. (2002). *Bringing words to life: robust vocabulary instruction*. New York : The Guildford Press.

Beck, I. L., McKeown, M. G., & Kucan, L. (2008). *Creating robust vocabulary: frequently asked questions and extended examples*. New York: Guilford Publications Inc.

Biemiller, A., & Boote, C. (2006). An effective method for building meaning vocabulary in primary grades. *Journal of Educational Psychology*, *98*(1), 44–62.

Bowyer-Crane, C., Snowling, M. J., Duff, F., Fieldsend, E., Carroll, J. M., Miles, J. N. V., & Hulme, C. (2008). Improving early language skills: differential effects of an oral language intervention and a phonology with reading intervention with language delayed young children. *Journal of Child Psychology and Psychiatry*, *49*, 422–432.

Bruner, J. S. (1978). The role of dialogue in language acquisition. In A. Sinclair, R. J. Jarvella & W. J. M. Levelt (eds), *The child's conception of language* (pp. 241–256). New York: Springer-Verlag.

Burgoyne, K., Kelly, J. M., Whiteley, H. E., & Spooner, A. (2009). The comprehension skills of children learning English as an additional language. *British Journal of Educational Psychology*, *79*(4), 735–747. doi: 10.1348/000709909X422530.

Cain, K., & Oakhill, J. V. (1999). Inference making ability and its relation to comprehension failure in young children. *Reading and Writing*, *11*(5–6), 489–507.

Cain, K., Oakhill, J., & Lemmon, K., (2005). The relation between children's reading comprehension level and their comprehension of idioms. *Journal of Experimental Child Psychology*, *90*, 65–87.

Cain, K., & Towse, A. S. (2008). To get hold of the wrong end of the stick: reasons for poor idiom understanding in children with reading comprehension difficulties. *Journal of Speech, Language, and Hearing Research*, *51*, 1538–1549.

Carroll, J. M., Bowyer-Crane, C., Duff, F., Hulme, C., & Snowling, M. J. (2011). *Developing language and literacy: effective intervention in the early years*. Chichester, UK: John Wiley & Sons, Ltd.

Clarke, P. J., Henderson, L. M., & Truelove, E. (2010). The poor comprehender profile: understanding and supporting individuals who have difficulties extracting meaning from text. *Advances in Child Development and Behaviour*, *39*, 79–129.

Clarke, P. J., Snowling, M. J., Truelove, E., & Hulme, C. (2010). Ameliorating children's reading comprehension difficulties: a randomised controlled trial. *Psychological Science, 21*, 1106–1116.

Corbett, P., & Corbett, P. (2005). *The story maker's chest: creative writing set*. Andover, UK: Philip & Tracey.

Davey, B. (1983). Think-aloud: modeling the cognitive processes of reading comprehension. *Journal of Reading, 27*(1), 44–47.

Department for Education and Skills (2006). Primary Framework for Literacy and Mathematics. http://www.niched.org/docs/the%20primary%20framework.pdf.

Duff, F., & Clarke, P. J. (2011). Practitioner review. Reading disorders: what are the effective interventions and how should they be applied and evaluated? *Journal of Child Psychology Psychiatry and Allied Disciplines, 52*, 3–12.

Farr, R., & Conner, J. (2004). Using Think-Alouds to Improve Reading Comprehension. Reading Rockets. http://www.readingrockets.org/article/102.

Fricke, S., Bowyer-Crane, C., Haley, A., Hulme, C., & Snowling, M. J. (2013). Building a secure foundation for literacy: an evaluation of a preschool language intervention. *Journal of Child Psychology and Psychiatry*. 54(3):280–90. doi: 10.1111/**jcpp**.12010

Garner, R. (1982). Resolving comprehension failure through text look backs: direct training and practice effects among good and poor comprehenders in grades six and seven. *Reading Psychology, 3*, 221–223.

Garner, R., Macready, G. B., & Wagoner, S. (1984). Readers' acquisition of the components of the text-lookback strategy. *Journal of Educational Psychology, 76*, 300–309.

Goncu, A., & Gauvain, M. (2011). Sociocultural approaches to educational psychology: theory, research, and application. In K. Harris, S. Graham & T. Urdan (eds), *APA educational psychology handbook*, Vol. *1, Theories, constructs and critical issues*. Washington, DC: American Psychological Association.

Gough, P. B., & Tunmer, W. E. (1986). Decoding, reading, and reading disability. *Remedial and Special Education, 7*, 6–10.

Hare, V. C., & Borchardt, K. M. (1984). Direct instruction of summarization skills. *Reading Research Quarterly, 20*, 62–78.

Hatcher, P. J., Hulme, C., & Ellis, A. W. (1994). Ameliorating early reading failure by integrating the teaching of reading and phonological skills: the phonological linkage hypothesis. *Child Development, 65*(1), 41–57.

Hatcher, P. J., Hulme, C., & Snowling, M. J. (2004). Explicit phoneme training combined with phonic reading instruction helps young children at risk of reading failure. *Journal of Child Psychology and Psychiatry, 45*(2), 338–358.

Hatcher, P. J., Götz, K., Snowling, M. J., Hulme, C., Gibbs, S., & Smith, G. (2006). Evidence for the effectiveness of the Early Literacy Support programme. *British Journal of Educational Psychology, 73*, 351–367.

Idol, L., & Croll, V. (1987). Story-mapping training as a means of improving reading comprehension. *Learning Disability Quarterly, 10*, 214–229.

Johnson-Glenberg, M. C. (2000). Training reading comprehension in adequate decoders/poor comprehenders: verbal vs. visual strategies. *Journal of Educational Psychology, 92*, 772–782.

Kintsch, W., & Rawson, K. A. (2005). Comprehension. In M. J. S. C. Hulme (ed.), *The science of reading: a handbook* (pp. 209–226). Malden, MA: Blackwell Publishing.

Kispal, A. (2008). *Effective teaching of inference skills for reading: literature review*. Nottingham: Department for Children, Schools and Families.

Legler, D. M. (1991). *Don't take it so literally! Reproducible activities for teaching idioms*. Phoenix, AZ: ECL Publications.

Lervåg, A., & Aukrust, V. G. (2010). Vocabulary knowledge is a critical determinant of the difference in reading comprehension growth between first and second language learners. *Journal of Child Psychology and Psychiatry, and Allied Disciplines*, *51*(5), 612–620.

McNamara, D. S. (2004). SERT: self-explanation reading training. *Discourse Processes*, *38*(1), 1–30.

Nation, K., Clarke, P., Marshall, C.M., & Durand, M. (2004). Hidden language impairments in children: parallels between poor reading comprehension and specific language impairment? *Journal of Speech, Language, and Hearing Research*, *47*, 199–211.

Nation, K., Cocksey, J., Taylor, J. S. H., & Bishop, D. V. M. (2010). A longitudinal investigation of early reading and language skills in children with poor reading comprehension. *Journal of Child Psychology and Psychiatry*, *51*(9), 1031–1039.

Nation, K., Marshall, C., & Altmann, G. T. M. (2003) Investigating individual differences in children's real-time sentence comprehension using language-mediated eye movements. *Journal of Experimental Child Psychology*, *86*, 314–329.

Nation, K., & Snowling, M. J. (1998a). Individual differences in contextual facilitation: evidence from dyslexia and poor reading comprehension. *Child Development*, *69*, 996–1011.

Nation, K., & Snowling, M. J. (1998b). Semantic processing and the development of word-recognition skills: evidence from children with reading comprehension difficulties. *Journal of Memory and Language*, *39*, 85–101.

Nation, K., Snowling, M. J., & Clarke, P. (2007). Dissecting the relationship between language skills and learning to read: semantic and phonological contributions to new vocabulary learning in children with poor reading comprehension. *Advances in Speech-Language Pathology*, *9*(2), 131–139.

National Reading Panel (2000). Teaching children to read: an evidence-based assessment of the scientific research literature on reading and its implications for reading instruction. Reports of subgroups. Rockville, MD: NICHD.

Neale, M. D. (1989). *The Neale analysis of reading ability*, Revised British Edition. Windsor, UK: NFER.

Oakhill, J. V., Hartt, J., & Samols, D. (2005). Comprehension monitoring and working memory in good and poor comprehenders. *Reading and Writing*, *18*, 657–686.

Oakhill, J. V., & Patel, S. (1991). Can imagery training help children who have comprehension problems? *Journal of Research in Reading*, *14*, 106–115.

Palinscar, A. S., & Brown, A. L. (1984). Reciprocal teaching of comprehension-fostering and comprehension-monitoring activity. *Cognition and Instruction*, *2*, 117–175.

Peters, E. E., Levin, J. R., McGivern, J. E., & Pressley, M. (1985). Further comparison of representational and transformational prose-learning imagery. *Journal of Educational Psychology*, *77*(2), 129–136.

Perfetti, C. A., Landi, N., & Oakhill, J. (2005). The acquisition of reading comprehension skill. In M. J. Snowing & C. Hulme (eds), *The science of reading: a handbook* (pp. 227–247). Oxford: Blackwell.

Raven, J. C. (1998). *Raven's standard progressive matrices*. San Antonio, TX: The Psychological Corp.

Ricketts, J., Bishop, D., & Nation, K. (2008). Investigating orthographic and semantic aspects of word learning in poor comprehenders. *Journal of Research in Reading*, *31*, 117–135.

Rogoff, B. (1990). *Apprenticeship in thinking: cognitive development in social context*. New York: Oxford University Press.

Seabrook, R., Brown, G. D. A., & Solity, J. E. (2005). Distributed and massed practice: from laboratory to classroom. *Applied Cognitive Psychology*, *19*(1), 107–122.

Sénéchal, M. (2006). Testing the home literacy model: parent involvement in kindergarten is differentially related to grade 4 reading comprehension, fluency, spelling, and reading for pleasure. *Scientific Studies of Reading, 10,* 59–87.

Snowling, M. J., Stothard, S. E., Clarke, P., Bowyer-Crane, C., Harrington, A., Truelove, E., Nation, K., & Hulme, C. (2009). York Assessment of Reading for Comprehension: Passage Reading. GL Assessment.

Stanovich, K. E. (1986). Matthew effects in reading: some consequences of individual differences in the acquisition of literacy. *Reading Research Quarterly, 21,* 360–364.

Torgerson, D., & Torgerson, C. J. (2008). *Designing and running randomised trials in health, education and the social sciences.* Basingstoke: Palgrave Macmillan.

Torgesen, J., Wagner, R., & Rashotte, C. (1997). *Test of word reading efficiency (TOWRE).* Austin, TX: Pro-Ed.

Vygotsky, L. S. (1962). *Thought and language.* (translated by E. Hanfmann & G. Vakar). Cambridge, MA: MIT Press.

Vygotsky, L. (1978). *Mind in society: the development of higher psychological processes.* Harvard University Press: Cambridge, Mass.

Wechsler, D. (1999). *Wechsler Abbreviated Scale of Intelligence (WASI).* San Antonio, TX: The Psychological Corp.

Wechsler, D. (2005). *Wechsler Individual Achievement Test - Second UK Edition (WIAT-IIUK).* London: Harcourt Assessment.

Yuill, N. (1998). Reading and riddling: the role of riddle appreciation in understanding and improving poor text comprehension in children. *Cahiers de Psychologie Cognitive, 17*(2), 313–342.

Yuill, N. (2009). The relation between ambiguity understanding and metalinguistic discussion of joking riddles in good and poor comprehenders: potential for intervention and possible processes of change. *First Language, 29*(1), 65–79.

Yuill, N., & Joscelyne, T. (1988). Effect of organisational cues and strategies on good and poor comprehenders' story understanding. *Journal of Educational Psychology, 80,* 152–158.

Yuill, N., & Oakhill, J. V. (1988). Effects of inference training on poor reading comprehension. *Applied Cognitive Psychology, 2,* 33–45.

Index

Printed and bound by CPI Group (UK) Ltd, Croydon, CR0 4YY